TODDLER DISCIPLINE

The Power of Positive Parenting and Healthy Communication In Your Toddler's Everyday Life

NATASHA BECKER

Copyright 2019 © Natasha Becker

Legal & Disclaimer

an illegal act irrespective of if it is done electronically or in print. This extends to creating a secondary or tertiary copy of the work or a recorded copy and is only allowed with an express written consent from the Publisher. All additional right reserved.

The information in the following pages is broadly considered to be a truthful and accurate account of facts, and as such any inattention, use or misuse of the information in question by the reader will render any resulting actions solely under their purview. There are no scenarios in which the publisher or the original author of this work can be in any fashion deemed liable for any hardship or damages that may befall them after undertaking information described herein.

Additionally, the information in the following pages is intended only for informational purposes and should thus be thought of as universal. As befitting its nature, it is presented without assurance regarding its prolonged validity or interim quality. Trademarks that are mentioned are done without written consent and can in no way be considered an endorsement from the trademark holder.

Table of Contents

Introduction

Discipline is an art; training human beings to adhere to certain behaviors through techniques such as positive reinforcement and unconditional love - which is affection without limitations or conditions. It is important to be creative in applying and using various discipline techniques with unconditional love because human beings react to discipline differently depending on different temperaments via nature and genetics, and different home environments via nurture. What works for one child may not work for another, in terms.

Without loving discipline, a toddler might eventually become an adult who runs amok, getting into trouble with no sense of right and wrong. This would be troublesome for his or her family, society and the undisciplined adult him or herself because deviant adults usually end up at odds with everybody else, given their unruly ways. The last thing anybody wants is for his or her child to end up on "Beyond Scared Straight," due to a lack of love and discipline.

The main task of the parent is to unconditionally love the child. You need to teach your child through unconditional love and positive discipline how to adopt healthy behaviors and habits that will help him or her thrive and progress in life. This training usually starts around the time the child is old enough to learn, and that can be anywhere from about six months old. As soon as a child is old enough to understand the words yes and no, the child is teachable. How you train and lovingly discipline your child is what makes the difference in his or her life, and with unconditional love, the child will thrive. Remember, unconditional love means accepting the child with all his or her imperfections as he or she is right now.

One aspect I am going to discuss in this book is getting a healthy balance in discipline, informed by unconditional love. If the parent is too strict and authoritarian in his or her style of parenting and discipline, the child might rebel and get into trouble of some kind. On the other hand, if the parent is too lenient and yielding, the child might think there would be no consequences for his or her actions. This could also lead to trouble for the child down the road. It would seem discipline is a very nuanced thing, depending on the individual child and his or her level of development. Be that as it may, unconditional love means loving and accepting the child. In other words, your love and care are consistent regardless of time, place or situation.

The most teachable and trainable moments are when the child is young in the formative years, in part because a toddler hasn't been all that influenced by the world quite yet. In addition, their minds are more open to suggestion as they are still growing and their behavior is more malleable and adaptable in comparison to most adults. Toddlers need more structure, guidance and loving but positive discipline in order to learn how to behave and to treat others in addition to themselves. Otherwise, a likely scenario might be similar to the "Daddy Daycare" movie where the daycare kids are running amok doing whatever whenever. It is when a positive role model steps in that makes all the difference to kids.

Positive parents employ positive parenting to teach and discipline their kids through love and guidance. Positive parenting is many things, but most importantly:

Positive parenting is the continual relationship of a parents(s) and a child or children that includes caring, teaching, leading, communicating, and providing for the needs of a child consistently and unconditionally (Seay et al., 2014, p 207.).

In other words, positive parenting is done through unconditional love for and discipline of the child through the actions the parents undertake to teach and raise said child into a fully accountable adult that can govern him or herself. This could include actions such as teaching the child to learn something like potty training through positive reinforcement techniques such as praising them for a job well done. Ultimately, positive parenting, unconditional love and discipline go hand-in-hand because all three give the toddler structure to learn from and to grow as an individual person. It is this loving discipline and unconditional care provided within positive parenting that is for the child's ultimate benefit, and not for the parents' benefit of making their lives easier through controlling the child. In short, approach is everything when it comes to the discipline of a child, especially a toddler.

Toddlers are sometimes known to throw temper tantrums, to hit other children, and to even test their boundaries and our patience. They can sometimes push us to the limit - and then some - through their emotional outbursts as well. In this book the parent will find the best answers to all his or her discipline woes with his or her toddler(s). This book will help the parent to not only positively discipline his or her toddler through unconditional love but to also grow closer to the child as a result of the relationship that develops as the parent works with him or her to ultimately build trust and confidence in each other along the way. As the parent applies the positive discipline techniques therein, the parent will find that his or her toddler will be more apt to work with him or her, to want to please the parent in his or her efforts, and to be more independent as a result. As a result of the parent's positive parenting and loving discipline techniques, the child will eventually have a great likelihood of becoming a responsible adult.

For example, if the toddler bites others, a tip is try to reduce his or her stress level through stress-reducing and tension-relieving activities such as playing soft music or offering him or her things that he or she can bite without hurting anybody else like teething rings. Positive guidance strategies and unconditional love can work when the parent expresses what behaviors are expected (better than expressing what you don't want). More specifically, use a firm but loving tone to let the toddler know biting is not allowed. Next, offer him or her a choice to either help the bitten child if both parties agree or to have the toddler sit quietly for a moment. It is important to talk to the toddler at the toddler's level when he or she bites and re-emphasize that it is not allowed. Finally, offer strategies the toddler can employ to avoid biting next time. Maybe even encourage him or her to use their words instead.

Once the child learns such things as not to bite, he or she will be able to socialize with other children his or her age in settings like a daycare, the YMCA or a playdate at a park. The child will also gain confidence in him or herself and in the ability to simply play with other children whilst being able to safely express feelings using words instead. As a result, the parent of said toddler can relax and enjoy the playdate as well, knowing the toddler has learned and applied a new set of skills. It would seem positive parenting and loving discipline are synonymous with focusing on positive outcomes, and they set the stage for future interactions down the road as well.

I can promise that with this book that the parent and the toddler will benefit from the application of unconditional love and the positive discipline techniques explained herein. The parent and the toddler will both be happier as a result, and more able to function on a day-to-day basis as the parent provides positive structure for his or her toddler to learn and to grow with unconditional love and proper discipline. In addition, the parent might also learn a thing or two from his or her toddler and be able to grow with him or her in such a way that the parent and the toddler become even closer. Other parents will be asking for parenting advice from the parent reading this book, as they witness how well-behaved the toddler is, too. The positive outcomes are plenty and numerous as the parent positively disciplines his or her child with unconditional love, patience, guidance and structure.

Do not wait to read this book because the toddler now and the adult in the future might suffer the consequences of the parent's inaction as a result. In short, the child's welfare and future is at stake. The toddler might not grow into the adult he or she is capable of becoming. The time to take action to ensure the well-being of the toddler is now. If you want your toddler to reap the emotional, social, and psychological rewards and benefits from positive parenting, unconditional love and discipline techniques, then invest in the toddler's present and future by investing in this book now. The parent will be able to see the difference in his or her toddler after applying only a few positive parenting and loving discipline techniques.

Positive changes in the toddler will be forthcoming no matter the situation or environment because applying the positive parenting and loving discipline techniques will set the stage for not only present interactions but future ones as well, as the toddler learns to navigate challenging situations first with the parent's help and unconditional love, and eventually on his or her own. It takes time, patience and unconditional love to repeatedly teach and to positively discipline the child but it will be worth it because once the child understands the lesson being taught, he or she will be able to adapt to numerous situations as that lesson is applied again and again. Maybe the child will even teach other children what he or she has learned as well. It is always a joy to witness the toddler's growth into a little person in his or her own right.

Clearly, the time to take action presents itself.

The toddler's mind, actions and reactions are still in his or her formative years, and the parent has the power to mold and lay the groundwork for present and future interactions, behaviors, thoughts and even relationships. All the toddler needs to succeed now and in the future is the parent's time, patience, unconditional love and the positive discipline techniques within this book. If the parent invests in his or her toddler today, the rewards will be endless as the parent witnesses his or her toddler growing as a little human being, and that is priceless in of itself.

Chapter One:
Brain Development and
The Wonder Years

We are always learning and growing regardless of our age and experience. This is even more true for toddlers because their brains grow very rapidly. New connections and brain cells amid neurons and synapses are constantly forming and developing and as a result, much growth and learning will take place during those first years. In fact, the toddler brain will quadruple in size by the time he or she graduates from preschool. It is during this time of learning and growth that we must take care in how we parent, teach, guide and lovingly discipline the child, because what we do in the present as parents can affect the child depending on style of discipline and nurturing. In fact, our main task as parents and caretakers is to love the child unconditionally no matter what. The resulting connections in the toddler's brain from this unconditional love and healthy discipline will lay the groundwork for future learning, interactions, beliefs and experiences in the child's life.

Structure is very important in the child's life. The child needs some kind of order to his or her day to function and thrive. Both unconditional love and structure will play a very important role in the toddler's development and growth because he or she will learn from these experiences as you teach, guide and discipline him or her. In fact, each new experience designs the toddler's brain as new neural connections take shape, thus wiring it to perform and think in certain ways beneficial to the toddler and his or her life. In addition, repetitive experiences that the toddler undergoes on a daily basis will reinforce these new neural connections that help mold and shape him or her into a self-governing and functioning individual. For example, a parent needs to repeatedly show the toddler how to take turns with other children when playing age-appropriate developmental games. That lesson will hopefully be remembered because of repetitive practice.

Toddler's Brain Development

Developmental cognitive neuroscience deals with how the mind affects the brain and vice versa. This is applicable to a toddler's developing and growing brain because how he or she thinks is directly tied in with the brain's stage of development and growth. For example, a toddler doesn't understand that incomplete reasoning results in decisions based on other than logical thought processes and reality. For example, what looks good or tastes good to eat may not actually be good for the toddler, like a hotdog or fries. If a toddler ate an unhealthy diet such as hotdogs and chips, his or her brain may not function as well as it could with a healthier diet which affects the development and health of the physical brain.

During the toddler years, the developing brain is very active in learning everything it can from the expression of emotions to socially acceptable behaviors. In addition, different parts of the toddler's brain are responsible for various aspects of learning information. For example, the frontal lobe of a toddler is capable of solving age-appropriate problems and expressing language, while the temporal lobe is known for speech, emotion and memory. Further, the parietal lobe focuses more on sensory experiences like the feel of a certain toy in the toddler's hand. The occipital lobe is more visual, helping the toddler to recognize things like specific shapes, numbers and letters. Finally, the cerebellum of a toddler is basically the basis of his or her physical capabilities like throwing a ball to his or her friend.

Furthermore, toddlers undoubtedly learn at a much faster rate than adults do, given the rapid development of their brain in the first few years. The abundant surplus of neurons and synapses form exceedingly fast in comparison to an adult brain that has already experienced functional fixedness that causes adults to see things in a more realistic light. In contrast, a toddler - and his or her brain - is more creative in how he or she views things because of the novelty of learning new things every day. It would seem that while the toddler brain is wired to creatively learn, the adult brain is wired to act and perform, in part given this functional fixedness. However, sometimes parents and caretakers need to remember what the world was like when they were a child in order to better understand

and comprehend their own offspring at such a young, impressionable age.

> **Quick Tip:** Since a toddler is more creative in how he or she views and learns things, perhaps offer the toddler creative activities to stimulate that part of the mind.

Toddlers are very impressionable and sensitive little human beings that need care, guidance and unconditional love to develop into self-governing and functioning individuals some day, with minds, thoughts and feelings of their own. In short, unconditional love through a responsive home environment can speed the progression of the development and growth of the toddler's brain.

Since the brain of a toddler isn't fully-formed

quite yet, temper tantrums and emotional outbursts may occur given lack of self-regulation skills and because the prefrontal cortex of a toddler is still developing causing emotions to not be regulated as well as an adult's experience of them. In other words, the construction of the brain is dependent on more than nature. The toddler's nurture, home environment and his or her experiences also come into play to support the healthy development of the toddler brain.

The emotional management capabilities of a two to three-year-old are dependent upon his or her synapses' health in the toddler brain. A toddler's synapses' health will be improved with the parent engaging his or her growing toddler in activities and experiences that strengthen healthy brain development and growth. As a result, the more the toddler will be able to adeptly regulate his or her emotions as a direct result. Healthy brain development is crucial in the toddler years because a bigger prefrontal cortex that controls executive functions like self-control, problem-solving and even personality will develop in the toddler brain, hopefully resulting in an adult who is emotionally stable, consistent and composed compared to otherwise. Likewise, emotional intelligence is not to be underestimated because this is what allows us to empathize with others, especially our growing toddlers.

On that note, the toddler's home environment needs to be nurturing and responsive for healthy brain development and growth to occur instead of stressful and indifferent which does nothing for the little one and his or her development and growth. In short, unconditional love during the early years is a must in the home environment. However, if the main environment the child is in happens to be full of negative stress, the toddler, as a result, might develop a bigger brain-stem which is accountable for the flight, fight or freeze response. This could result in the toddler becoming accustomed to handling stressful situations in such a way that he or she overreacts to any little stress, thus overstressing the stressor itself. A toddler's home environment is everything because it is where the toddler's brain becomes wired to handle things later in life as an adult.

Quick Tip: Although a toddler's home environment is important to his or her brain development, it is also crucial to expose the toddler to various environments to ensure the child's brain development doesn't come to a standstill from being in just one environment.

Ways To Support Healthy Brain Development

The parent should practice feeding the toddler the right foods and diet to help and promote his or her brain formation and function as well. For example, some foods that can help support the healthy development of neural connections in a toddler's brain are fish, peanut butter and nuts like walnuts to name a few. This is due to some fat being needed to support and construct the myelination in a toddler's brain which is an endeavor in which the neural connections are sheathed in a fatty material to help them travel faster and more efficiently. In other words, some fat is necessary in the child's diet for structuring and wiring the brain. Other foods which also help to support healthy brain development are, of course, fruits like berries and oranges, vegetables like spinach and broccoli and whole grains like oatmeal and wheat pasta. The parent should model for the toddler which foods to eat by eating them him or herself first, as children will mirror and replicate what mom, dad or the caretaker does regarding eating a healthy well-rounded diet.

Quick Tip: In order to help your child's brain develop and grow properly with a healthy diet of fruits, vegetables, meats, dairy, and grains, perhaps try disguising veggies and other healthy foods as fast food or a sweet treat if he or she is a picky eater. For example, cut baby carrots into what looks like french fries or maybe even use a Spiralizer to disguise veggies as tasty pasta.

Parents and caretakers can also help the toddler to develop healthy brain function by giving him or her cognitively stimulating activities to do which engage the toddler's abilities and skills for his or her age level and development stage. For example, social activities can improve brain development and growth through the enhancement of the toddler's language skills when in social settings with his or her peers. One example of a social activity could be taking the child on a play date so he or she can engage with other children. To explain, when the parents or other children talk to the toddler, his or her language center in the brain learns that particular vocalization through repetition of it. One or two syllable words are assimilated and picked up rather fast by the toddler. This is when the parents or the caretakers of the toddler model the words and language first to improve communication and his or her toddler's language skills through the means of simply talking and conversing with him or her. Social connections encourage communication and conversation no matter the age or development stage.

Another action parents and caretakers of the child can take to encourage healthy brain development in the toddler is to consider enrolling him or her in a daycare, preschool or some other social setting. This can aid and help the toddler in so many areas such as social and cognitive development and growth and the improved abilities that result from it. For example, my mom kept me at home when I was a toddler instead of putting me in a daycare or some other social setting with other kids in my own age group and development level. As a result, by the time I got to the first year of kindergarten, I was so shy and quiet that I had to repeat kindergarten to catch up developmentally with my peers. I guess I just wasn't ready socially or cognitively to learn and to function with other kids quite yet that first year. Although it is a personal choice to put the toddler into a daycare or another social setting like preschool, it is the toddler who will benefit the most from that choice.

An additional positive choice to support and encourage healthy brain development and growth is to give the toddler plenty of opportunity and room to run, to play and to exercise. This is vital because a healthy body results in a healthy brain and vice versa. In addition, daily exercise can also help develop those neural connections in the toddler's brain in such a way that healthy habits and routines are formed for life through repetitive physical activity, whether that be running or climbing the jungle gym. It is important to start them while they're young and more open to suggestion. For example, when my son was a toddler, I took him to many local parks in the hopes of encouraging him to play and to be active via simply moving around with other children in his age group. I still recall him running around the park with other kids in a game of hide and seek. Yet along with the exercising of the body also comes the exercising of the brain itself.

Supporting the development and growth of healthy brain function and the toddler's mind is some more cognitively stimulating and age-appropriate intellectual activities such as learning the ABCs and counting numbers. Another idea is to have your toddler put back together a puzzle with big colorful pieces that he or she dumped all over the kitchen table. This activity will focus on the toddler recognizing shapes, while other activities could focus on the toddler recognizing colors. The parent could sing along with his or her toddler to a song they know and heard on Sesame Street, Sprouts or some other age-appropriate program on television. Another age-appropriate way to develop your toddler's brain function and mind is to have them identify sounds and noises like a cat meowing or a car honking. My son used to like the noise of a fire engine and a squad car rushing by the house when he was a toddler. The intellectual or cognitive activities you can engage in with your toddler are endless and fun!

There are many ways to support a healthy brain development, with the most relevant being:

- A healthy diet
- Cognitive stimulation
- Social setting
- Exercise
- Intellectual activities

Brain Development and Memory

If the toddler is experiencing healthy brain development and growth, then he or she also experiences explicit memory during the first three years of his or her life. This explicit memory is a combination of episodic memory and semantic memory. Episodic memory is a remembrance of experiences while semantic memory is tied into a remembrance of facts like those present in language and numbers. This combination leading to the explicit memory of a toddler allows him or her to remember things like his or her birthday party or what the letter "a" looks like

Other kinds of memory developing in a toddler's brain are:

- Short-Term
- Working
- Long-Term
- Autobiographical

The short-term memory of a toddler is not very functional yet, given the lack of development of the prefrontal cortex until about ages three or four. The toddler's brain cannot hold or store information for very long. This directly affects the working memory of the toddler because since he or she cannot hold onto information very efficiently, the toddler will need many repetitions to learn something new like a teachable discipline moment. Repetitive practice of a healthy discipline lesson is sometimes necessary to drive the point home for a toddler to understand it. Be that as it may, every child or toddler is different in terms of development and growth of the brain given nurture and nature. I cannot stress the importance of unconditional love enough, regardless of the environment the toddler is functioning in.

The long-term memory of a toddler is more tied in with his or her autobiographical memory because toddlers more strongly remember personal experiences. These personal experiences are made up of explicit memory in which the toddler's brain makes a combination of episodic and semantic memory. This kind of memory is absolutely vital for a growing and evolving toddler because it allows him or her to remember events like positive discipline, locations like grandma's house and people like mom and dad that help define who the toddler is. The toddler then has a stronger sense of self as a result of that autobiographical memory. In addition, the toddler might even feel more confident with a stronger sense of self and be able to relate to other kids his or her age more easily and efficiently. In short, it is good for the toddler to have as many memories as possible to pull from to identify with, compared to otherwise.

This is why a positive, loving and responsive environment makes such a big difference as to the development and growth of a toddler's brain and mind. The toddler's brain development will come to fruition much faster and easier in such an environment where the toddler is loved consistently and unconditionally no matter what. This progressive brain development via nurture and experiences will help the toddler in many areas of his life now and in the future. For example, the toddler, some day, as a self-governing adult will be more likely to procure a satisfying career with his or her strong brain and mind. In addition, since the function of the mind and body are connected, the toddler will also benefit from a healthy brain by having a healthier body to support it. Everything is interconnected and this combination will some day produce a healthy, stable adult that will be able to think and act for him or herself through self-government of both the body and the mind. In fact, you almost have to be intentionally mindful these days as a parent or caretaker, especially with the distraction of electronics, to produce a human being with a mind strong enough to think on its own without the addition of electronics.

However, electronic like tablets and laptops can also enhance the toddler's brain and mind within reason. To explain, it is okay to employ these electronics as aids to teach the toddler, but not as babysitters to pacify the toddler. Besides, pacifying the toddler with a cellphone doesn't really help him or her to learn, given that sometimes one must step out of his or her comfort zone to learn something new. It is important as parents to be selective when presenting electronics as teaching aids because all that screen-time is not good for a young, developing mind. This is because the toddler can become irritable and get headaches to name a few ailments. In addition, the toddler with too much screen-time might be less reliant on him or herself to think and learn, due to the fact that technology these days does much of the work for us there.

Yet if the parent is going to employ electronics as a teaching aid, it is highly recommended to invest in Leapfrog. These electronics are more kid-friendly and age appropriate. In addition, they are more designed to assist the child in learning specific to the stage of development and even the subject. Leapfrog electronics and teaching aids are very helpful because they focus on a child's needs and make it fun.

Learning about the developing toddler brain itself, what it is capable of, and how those capabilities can be nurtured through environment, diet and exercise is clearly valuable. The physical brain and how it works are directly affected by everyday activities, which is why it is vital to ensure the toddler has a healthy environment to thrive in. Ensuring good brain health for your toddler now will promote good health in all areas of his or her life.

Chapter Two:
The Importance of Positive Parenting and Disciplining

Positive parenting and discipline are a shift in thinking about parenting that focuses more on what the child can do and learn with his or her skills and capabilities in their given stage of development in comparison to what the child cannot do at their age. This shift in focus when it comes to parenting and discipline is in part due to past definitions of parenting and discipline paying more attention to correcting the child and his or her behavior instead of showing him or her the right way to do things through positive structure, guidance and unconditional love. In fact, positive parenting and caretaking is a way to restructure not only the physical brain and mind but also the lifestyle of both parent(s) and the toddler through adopting and learning new techniques to guide your toddler whilst giving him or her the structure and love he or she needs to thrive.

Yet it can be challenging to restructure our parenting style and habits given how we were raised ourselves by our own parents or caretakers. Certain parenting habits become so ingrained that we do them without even thinking about them, like letting the toddler use his or her outside voice while in the house. There are plenty of examples of our parents being lenient, yielding and permissive with us when we were children, but if parents are too strict, children might not have enough leeway to be children if they have a life full of too many rules. It is easy to repeat the same style of parenting and caretaking with our toddlers. It just becomes second nature after years of conditioning. Still, it clearly takes a conscious effort to not repeat history with our own kids, while it also takes a conscious attempt to learn something new regarding positive parenting and disciplining.

Quick Tip: It is okay to disagree with our parents concerning the way we raise our own children. In fact, it is sometimes necessary to develop new habits as a positive parent and disciplinarian.

Your job as a parent and as a caretaker is to love the child no matter what. It is important to be proactive as much as possible with positive parenting and discipline of the toddler instead of being reactive to the situation without thought and consideration of the little person that needs your guidance and love. Positive parenting and discipline might take some effort on your part as the parent, but it will be worth it when you witness the toddler growing and learning as an individual in his or her own right.

It is important to remember that parenting is only done with the understanding that your main job as the parent is to unconditionally love your child first and foremost; that love, empathy and heart have to be there. Discipline without love is like joining the military in which drill sergeants scream at you to get the point across. Yet all love and no discipline will have a child doing whatever he or she wants without fear of reprisal or consequences, leading to the child learning the hard way in the real world later in life. In short, act on your child's behalf with unconditional love now while the window of opportunity presents itself.

Parenting can be challenging, as it requires repetitive practice. It is an undertaking in which you and your toddler will be learning together about new methods and techniques as you repeatedly attempt over and over to guide your toddler with structure and unconditional love. It is this structure that will allow your toddler to grow and to learn what is appropriate and socially acceptable and what is not. In fact, it would seem less-than-positive parenting shapes children into people that may cause social problems like domestic violence. The last thing any parent wants is to learn that his or her adult child has committed a crime due to lack of discipline earlier on. This is part of the reason positive parenting and discipline are so valuable.

Another reason positive parenting is so important is that happier and more productive members of society are created, who are more industrious and willing to devote themselves to something worthwhile like a pursuit of some kind like parenting or a career. Happy people are more active, in part because they spend less time and energy worrying about things out of their control. As a result, happy people are more focused and energetic because they have better mental, emotional and physical health. Parenting and disciplining with positivity and love is priceless.

This style of parenting fortifies the heart of our culture, the familial unit. When a family employs these new techniques and methods, a positive way of life envelopes said familial unit and everybody else they come into contact with throughout their lives. This has the effect of creating other positive familial structures within society, whether that be at work or otherwise. Clearly, upbeat parenting and discipline can apply to more than one situation or societal unit. It would seem this style of parenting and correcting the children structures society on a bigger level.

Quick Tip: Parenting and disciplining multiple children requires creativity on the parent's part because every child is different emotionally, mentally, and physically. As a result, the child may require various methods of positive parenting and disciplining more suited to his or her learning style, temperament, and ability.

Discipline Ages and Stages

Positive parenting and loving discipline have to start somewhere. The question is at what age do we start to unconditionally love and discipline our children? According to the current research, it is okay to start discipline at about four to seven months. At this tender age, the baby starts to literally grasp and tug at everything he or she can, for it is their natural instinct. However, if your little one pulls at your necklace and accidentally breaks it, simply put the baby down for a moment instead of yelling "no". It may take a while, but the message will get across to him or her.

In addition, discipline at about seven to twelve months is a more of a challenge because the baby is now more active and getting into just about everything he or she can. Now would be a good time to put away objects the baby can inadvertently hurt him or herself with; objects like a pencil or even keys laying on the end of a table. Even if the object doesn't seem like it would hurt the baby if he or she grabbed it, think again. Everything is fair game to your baby because they are exploring the environment with his or her newfound ability to crawl and scoot. Be that as it may, discipline at this age is simple enough, distract and redirect. Even a change in your tone of voice will eventually drive the point home as well.

Moving on, unconditional love and discipline at about twelve to eighteen months is more demanding because it seems no matter how many times you patiently and lovingly instruct the child not to be loud with his or her vocal abilities, the growing toddler just doesn't seem to understand and comprehend what you are asking of him or her. This is in part because toddlers don't quite yet possess self-control. In addition, a toddler's working memory is not quite all there yet. Continue to lovingly and patiently instruct the child anyway. Perhaps even model the behavior you do want and in about another year or so, the child should come around with the help of those repetitive discipline lessons.

Positive parenting and discipline at about eighteen to twenty-four months is about helping the toddler with autonomy. Since the growing and evolving toddler cannot always vocalize his or her strong feelings as part of that autonomy, frustration can result in acting out with outbursts and temper tantrums. Instead of reacting to the toddler when he or she cries out, patiently help him or her use words instead. Perhaps vocalize what it is the frustrated toddler is trying to express in your own words. This display of positive parenting will show the toddler that you empathize with him or her and as a result, a stronger bond will develop between you two.

On that note, positive parenting discourages

spanking because it teaches the toddler that bigger people can hit smaller people. This is obviously wrong because it is only a power play to get the child to listen and behave through shock and fear. It also sends mixed messages because while the parent is supposed to love the child unconditionally, hitting another is also quite the opposite of love. Unconditional love is not about manipulating the child through fear. Instead, unconditional love, together with positive parenting and discipline are about treating the child as a person in his or her own right via the golden rule which is "do unto others as you would have them do unto you".

As already discussed, parenting obviously needs love and healthy discipline. Healthy discipline is much different from unhealthy discipline in that healthy discipline focuses on positive outcomes for the toddler whereas unhealthy discipline produces negative outcomes for everyone involved. In addition, if you unconditionally love your child no matter what and even if, it would seem a positive parent and caretaker would want the best for that child in comparison to otherwise. In short, healthy discipline is a much-needed ingredient to produce a healthy, well-adjusted individual that can possibly someday return the favor when the parent of said individual is too advanced in years to care for him or herself. In this vein, positive parenting with love and discipline is the glue that holds the family together through generations.

Discipline Tips for Parents

In any case, in order to discipline a toddler in a healthy manner, sometimes we must isolate the emotion from the act of disciplining itself. Otherwise, the emotions the parent(s) feels could overwhelm and escalate the discipline into something other than healthy like abuse. This is what the parent wants to avoid at all costs because the child will pay the ultimate price when he or she has trouble separating emotions and risks repeating history in disciplining his or her own child. Instead, if the parent can remain calm and collected while disciplining the child in a healthy manner, the toddler will not only feel safe but also reassured that the parent still loves him or her unconditionally no matter what and even if.

What the parent also wants to do to discipline his or her toddler in a healthy manner is to think versus fight. This means that you proactively consider healthy discipline options and choices instead of reactively fighting or arguing with one another. Besides, fighting and arguing usually lead to nowhere. On that note, your toddler will mirror your behavior and repeat it when put in a similar situation, or when you least expect it. Therefore, it is very important to employ your mind during healthy discipline moments because this will lead to a more positive and optimal outcome for the toddler, like eventually learning to work it out for him or herself.

Quick Tip: In order to think versus fight with your toddler, try using a quick memory trick like a mnemonic device such as a short poem or phrase to avoid fighting with the toddler. Memory tricks will help you handle things better because you will be more able to think under stress.

Healthy discipline also includes consequences for one's actions and empathy. The empathy to understand what your toddler is going through given the consequences you enacted show you care about him or her. It shows you care about the toddler's welfare and well-being. Yet caring about the toddler's well-being also requires the parent or caretaker to enforce the consequences as well. Otherwise, the toddler might think he or she can do whatever he or she wants without experiencing the consequences firsthand. This would make for a very presumptuous toddler and human being without limits. Clearly, healthy discipline and positive parenting include setting limits on what your toddler can and can't do via socially acceptable behaviors.

Another balance to remember in order to discipline your toddler in a healthy manner is control versus maturity. This is easier said than done with toddlers because they are sometimes out of control with their occasional emotional outbursts. Yet the more a toddler can demonstrate some maturity for his or her age and developmental level, the more control he or she will have in making choices for him or herself, compared to the parent(s) choosing everything for the toddler when he or she is out of control. Either way, it is important to consider how mature a toddler can possibly be given individual development. In other words, healthy discipline begins with knowledge of the child's possible maturity level given things such as brain development.

Healthy discipline clearly focuses on choices and accountability for those choices. If you give your child choices stemming from enforcing healthy discipline strategies, he or she will ultimately have to undergo the consequences of those choices, whether good or bad. This will lead to hopefully more sound choices on the part of the toddler next time the opportunity arises for him or her to decide which avenue to take. This teaches the child responsibility for his or her actions in a positive and healthy way, compared to forcing them to behave through manipulation and control.

There are many discipline tips out there but the most valuable ones for positive parenting and healthy discipline are:

- Isolate emotion from the act of discipline
- Think versus fight
- Enact consequence with empathy
- Balance control with maturity
- Teach accountability for choices

Clearly, positive parenting and healthy discipline are about showing the child you love him or her through your positive actions. Your main task as the parent is to love the child no matter what This is why it is so important to employ unconditional love with healthy discipline and structure for the child's age and development level. It shows the child you care. Yet it is also important to consider that not every child develops the same skills at the same growth rate. Every toddler is a unique individual with his or her own traits and characteristics.

A toddler's job is to have fun and to learn as much about him or herself and the world as he or she can due to age and development. Learning is related to the word discipline because it implies the acquisition of new information itself. In other words, even the word discipline implies a positive learning experience and process, instead of the negative rap that is often associated with it. For example, the learning of a medium of art can be described as a discipline. Discipline with love for the toddler is most definitely a learning process for your little one, and sometimes even for the parent(s), too.

That being said, healthy discipline with love is more about the child and less about the parents. This is because the love and discipline you show and demonstrate to your toddler are to benefit the toddler and his or her life now and in the future as an adult. Sure, it would be easy to discipline your little one for your benefit of control and peace of mind, but maybe that isn't the best outlook. Discipline with love has to be centered on the toddler him or herself, and not you the parent. After all, the love of your little one is what prompted you to invest in him or her by researching this book.

Positive parenting using healthy discipline with love is a choice. A positive choice to guide and structure your toddler's life in a beneficial and constructive manner. Likewise, when you discipline your toddler, it is important to give them choices that will someday shape him or her into a stable, well-adjusted individual in society.

Two choices are sufficient to give to your toddler when you discipline him or her in a healthy manner because it convinces the toddler that he or she has control over their own life and the choices in it. In addition, too many choices can be overwhelming for your little one.

The choices you give your toddler should reflect the task you give him or her. For example, you want your toddler to help you pick up his or her toys at the end of the day. You give your toddler two options or choices with this task; either pick them up or don't pick them up. In addition, the parent should be okay with both of the options because either way, the child will learn something. If your toddler chooses to pick up the toys him or herself, the toddler will learn to be more accountable for his or her actions resulting from taking out all the toys from the toybox. If your toddler chooses not to pick them up, then he or she still learns there will be a consequence for that choice, like no dessert after supper. Either way, your little one will eventually understand that the better choice involves mommy or daddy not picking up the slack for him or her.

It is important for the parents to feel like they have choices too when it comes to the loving discipline of their child. The choices themselves can either be positive or negative. Positive choices like reinforcing the toddler's behavior and negative choices like decreasing the child's behavior send a message to the child that it is up to them to decide. Choices are key to positive parenting and to unconditionally loving the toddler no matter what and even if.

Positive and Negative Reinforcement and Punishment plus Response Cost

One positive choice the parent can make is to reinforce the toddler's behavior with positive reinforcement. To explain, positive reinforcement adds something valuable the child wants in order to increase a behavior. For example, if your toddler eats his or her vegetables, then the toddler gets to play longer with his or her friends. In short, positive reinforcement basically adds something the child wants to strengthen his or her initial behavior.

On the other hand, negative reinforcement detracts something the child doesn't want in order to reinforce his or her behavior. For example, if the toddler brushes his or her teeth without being told to, perhaps take away one of his or her chores for the day. This will result in the toddler being more willing to take care of his or her dental hygiene. Reinforcement is key to getting the child to comply with what you ask of him or her. It strengthens the child's behavior and even the bond between parent and child. This happens because the child and the caretaker grow closer through their shared experiences of positive parenting and discipline.

However, punishment is a more difficult subject to tackle because of the negative connotation it has, given past definitions of corporal punishment. Corporal punishment is not recommended in positive parenting because oftentimes the parent loses control when they are spanking the child in anger. Instead, healthy punishment detracts something the child would prefer to keep like screen time on the tablet or going to the park to play with friends. Taking away something the toddler wants will decrease his or her behavior.

For example, if the toddler loves to go to the park, but doesn't comply with your request to put on his or her coat, then the toddler doesn't go to the park.

Punishment can also be positive because it adds something the child doesn't want in order to decrease behavior like a penalty of some kind. For example, your toddler grabs a toy from his or her friend on their playdate. The parent could give the child a time out to sit quietly with mommy or daddy instead of letting the child play with his or her friend. Positive punishment could also include giving the child a stern explanation as to why his or her favorite toy has been taken away for hitting his or her friend. Positive punishment is a deterrent to misbehaving.

Additionally, misbehaving can be discouraged through response cost. Response cost is incorporating a reinforcer to increase behavior with a punishment to decrease behavior. For example, say you need to go to the store to do the grocery shopping for the week, and your toddler doesn't want to go. The parent could give the toddler a baggie with some money in it to buy a toy or a sweet treat of some kind. This is the reinforcer. If the toddler misbehaves at the grocery store, mom or dad could take away some of those dollar bills, thus decreasing the child's likelihood of getting a small toy or a sweet treat. This is the punishment for misbehaving. Thus, the cost the child pays is directly tied in with his or her response to the task at hand. Lastly, you allow the toddler to get the toy or sweet treat or have him or her save it for next time if there isn't enough money left via their response to the task at hand.

There are many ways to condition a child to behave appropriately. Some of those discipline methods include:

- Positive reinforcement
- Negative reinforcement
- Negative punishment
- Positive punishment
- Response cost

Misbehaving is a common occurrence for toddlers because at such a young, impressional age, they are still learning how to behave. In addition, a toddler's working memory isn't the same as an adult's working memory, so toddlers need repetition in order to understand what it is you are trying to get across to them. A toddler might behave according to what he or she observes in the demeanor you are projecting. For example, if you appear upset with your body language and words, the toddler might be more inclined to act up in response. However, if the parent projects a cool and collected appearance, the toddler might just behave well because he or she will recognize they aren't getting to you with their antics. A calm mind and body are essential if you want to positively parent and discipline your child with unconditional love no matter what.

Another helpful tip to positively parent and lovingly discipline your child in a healthy manner is to apply the consequence in a positive way. This means not giving the child an ultimatum that sounds harsh and final but explaining to the child that when you do this, we will do that. Frame the consequence in such a way that it doesn't seem like a negative thing. This is very important because the child will feel like he or she isn't really getting punished. It's almost like reverse psychology in a way.

Speaking of psychology, a useful key is to remember the positivity vector. This is all about looking more at the positive side of things. It helps you positively parent and discipline your child because it focuses on creating happiness through comparison of what is and of what could be. It looks at things in a more creative light. For example, when evaluating your parenting in purely a lateral way and just see things as they are from your perspective, things might seem less than optimal, that is until you compare your parenting situation to another parenting situation that is worse. Then you start to feel better. On the other end of the spectrum, when you compare your parenting situation to something better, you begin to feel less than positive.

However, when you consider what is to be, what positive outcomes could occur, you are creatively using your imagination to improve the situation by considering the happier and healthier choices that lead to better outcomes in the future. For example, when you witness your child misbehaving, you can imagine what could be if you applied the actions within this book. Then you feel better with positive emotions like hope for the future. On the other hand, if your child is already behaving well and you imagine a worst-case scenario, you might be inclined to feel less than positive. Clearly, when parents creatively apply their imagination to the situation, they are creating a more positive experience and future outcome for themselves and their toddler. Positivity in parenting is everything!

Chapter Three:
How To Set Limits Without Damaging My Kids And Why Toddlers Need Boundaries

Setting limits with our children is never easy. This is because emotions and feelings can cloud our judgment sometimes, especially when we are disciplining our own kids. Oftentimes we can get upset or lose our patience and temper when we are trying to manage misbehavior. This is when we must take a step back and attempt to objectively re-assess the situation as best we can because even - especially - in the heat of the moment, a mom or dad must strategize how best to lovingly discipline and set limits with his or her child in a loving way without compromising the child's well-being or their sense of self. This is a challenging task even with the most experienced parents and caretakers because every child is different when it comes to setting and enforcing limits. In addition, just when you think your toddler is behaving well, his or her curiosity reinvents the rules of the game once more. This is when you try a new approach with creativity and love. After all, there is more than one way to get the point across to your little one.

How to Set Limits

It is also important to focus more on what you *can* control as a parent when setting and enforcing limits in comparison to what you *can't* control, like the child's emotional outburst or reactions to the limits set by mom or dad. The child's reactions aren't always a result of the limits themselves, but possibly more a reaction as to how those limits are enforced by mom or dad. In other words, approach is everything when it comes to setting and enforcing limits in a loving way with your little one. If you yell angrily in frustration when enforcing limits with your toddler, of course he or she is going to react to your heated reaction. Yet if mom or dad can remain calm, cool and collected, perhaps the toddler will also remain the same by mirroring his or her parent's or caretaker's emotional projection. As a result, the toddler will be more likely to go along with mom's or dad's requests to behave well. On that note, it is important to be kind to your toddler when setting and enforcing limits. Just imagine how you would feel if somebody yelled at you to do something. How would you feel as a result? In short, try to put yourself in the same situation as your toddler, and you will be less inclined to react and more likely to act instead when it comes to setting and enforcing limits.

Setting limits also requires you to be clear and specific with your requests, rather than being vague and ambiguous with your child. For example, instead of kindly asking your child to be nice to his or her little brother or sister, perhaps try to be more specific and ask the child to give the little guy a hug instead. This request is clear and more defined than the adjective "nice". In addition, perhaps the toddler is too inexperienced with language to understand what the word "nice" really means, because it is less straightforward than a simple directive you give to him or her. It is important to talk to your toddler at his or her level in a language he or she can understand. In addition, toddlers need more time and experience to understand and comprehend the complexities of language first. However, what toddlers do understand is usually modeled by their caretakers first in a loving way around language and otherwise.

Quick Tip: In order to convince a child to incorporate new limits and rules him or herself, be a consistent example of how you want your child to behave and act. Children often look to their parents for help and guidance.

Consistency is also key when setting limits with a toddler. If you set a clear limit and he or she doesn't listen at the first opportunity given to comply, the parent should consistently and repeatedly follow through on the consequences. This is because otherwise, the child will not take mom or dad seriously enough to abide by what is asked of him or her. This could lead to problems for the toddler when he or she becomes an adult. On the other hand, the more consistent the parent is in enforcing the consequences, the more likely the toddler will listen to mom or dad as his or her words become worth every penny.

The last thing a parent should want is for his or her toddler to blow him or her off and do what the toddler wants anyway, all because mom or dad wasn't consistent in following through when enforcing the consequences.

However, setting limits with toddlers can be easy enough when mom or dad follow a few simple suggestions. For example, the parents could put the brakes on their toddler's misbehavior before it even starts. What this means is to put something dangerous to the toddler away out of his or her reach before he or she can get into it him or herself. For example, if mom or dad has the remote control out on the couch somewhere, perhaps move it to higher ground like the kitchen table so the toddler won't be able to change the channel on you or stick the remote in his or her mouth. Obviously, it would be wise to toddler-proof your home environment because then mom or dad will have less reason to discipline the little one.

Distracting the toddler also works when trying to redirect his or her behavior. For example, the parent or the caretaker could invite the toddler to play with his or her favorite toy, especially when the toddler is loudly banging together the pans that he or she found in the cupboard. If you want your toddler to shift gears on what he or she is currently doing or getting into, then side-track the little one with another activity or object. This works because the toddler has a short attention span anyway, and he or she usually won't remember what they were doing the moment before you distracted him or her with something else.

As you know, setting limits can be challenging when the toddler is exhausted to begin with, so monitor his or her amount of sleep on a nightly basis. Toddlers usually need more sleep than adults do, about two to four more hours a night.

In addition, toddlers also need to take naps during the day. I still remember when my mom, who ran a daycare in her home, had all the daycare kids lay down on their cots for some shut-eye after lunch. All of this importance on a toddler's sleep routine or schedule ties into setting limits, too. This is because if your little one is tired anyway, he or she will be more likely to misbehave and have a tantrum when mom or dad asks him or her to do or not to do something. In addition, the one main task of sleep is vital to the toddler's behavior and mood. Even adults get cranky and misbehave from lack of sleep every now and then.

Ignoring your child when he or she misbehaves can also be a wise strategy because if he or she doesn't get a reaction from you to begin with, the toddler might be less likely to act up. Having mom or dad's attention is priceless to the child, so if you look the other way, he or she will be less inclined to misbehave and act out of turn. Try not to look at the child because the second you give attention to his or her behavior, you will reinforce what the toddler is doing in the first place. I know this technique may sound indifferent but I assure you that down the road when the child is an adult, he or he will be less likely to misbehave, because the toddler as an adult won't get the wrong kind of attention for it.

Setting limits with the child is necessary for him or her to become a healthy, stable and self-governing adult someday. Yet this will be less likely to happen if the child does not have consequences for their misbehavior. The caretaker must begin by implementing a rule for the toddler to follow like picking up his or her toys before going outside to play with his or her friends. If the child doesn't abide by the rules mom or dad set, that is when mom or dad must warn the child with a consequence, thus teaching cause and effect to the child as well. If the child still doesn't listen, immediately enforce the consequence. Do not hesitate, the parent has to be unwavering when setting the consequence. If the child senses your hesitation even for a second, he or she might just take advantage of the situation somehow and even escalate their behavior.

Another technique mom or dad can try for setting and enforcing limits with his or her toddler is to try modified time-outs depending on the age and developmental level of the child and the misbehavior itself. For example, if your toddler pulls your hair when holding him or her in your lap, perhaps put the toddler down for a few minutes and exclaim "no" in a firm tone. The child will eventually get the message with repetitive practice. It might take a bit of time before the child associates the time out with the misbehavior, but eventually, he or she will get the message loud and clear.

Setting and enforcing limits with the child can also be accomplished by doing more than exclaiming the word "no" to your little one all the time, although it is easier to do for many parents. For example, instead of just reacting with the vocalization of the word "no" when the child misbehaves or acts out of turn, perhaps try to suggest an alternative to what he or she wants to do. If the toddler insists on climbing the furniture inside the house, perhaps give him or her the alternative of going to the park to climb on the jungle gym instead. This will mitigate the situation for both the toddler and the parent as well.

It is also important that the word "no" isn't overused to the point that the toddler doesn't take it as seriously when you do say it in an emergency.

Quick Tip: To implement healthy limits and boundaries for the toddler, perhaps have an older child close to the toddler's age model the behavior and explain why it is necessary in a language the toddler understands. This will help with the toddler accepting the new limit easier given it is a peer and not an authority figure like mom or dad.

Clearly, there are many ways to set limits with toddlers, but some of the more important ones to remember are:

- Focus on what you can control
- Be clear and specific
- Be consistent
- Stop the misbehavior before it starts
- Distract
- Monitor sleep
- Pay less attention to the child's misbehavior
- Enforce consequences
- Try modified time-outs
- Don't use the word "no" all the time

Toddlers need limits because it helps to create healthy boundaries for them to keep them safe. These healthy boundaries help to define what the child can and cannot do through repeatedly implementing limits and consequences if and when necessary. In addition, age-appropriate boundaries help the child to understand what is expected of his or her behavior for that specific age and developmental level. Toddlers also learn what is socially acceptable by their caretaker's implementation of the limits, thus creating healthy boundaries in time with practice. Likewise, boundaries may even help us adults from time to time to discern right from wrong sometimes as well.

Yet toddlers still want to be independent because it is important to them to be able to make their own choices when they can in order to help them feel like they have their own agency and volition as individuals in their own right. They are constantly working on personal autonomy as they explore and sometimes even test those limits and boundaries we have set for them to keep them safe and sound. It is when toddlers test the boundaries set for them, however, that we as parents and caretakers must sometimes make choices for them. For example, when the child throws a screaming fit because he or she doesn't want to do something you have asked of him or her. This is when you step in and make that choice for the toddler in part because they are not developed enough yet to make it on their own as a two-year-old child still learning and maturing.

When to Choose for the Toddler

In other words, two to three-year-old children sometimes need mom or dad's help to decide what is best for them in order to be well-adjusted and stable little people because toddlers are constantly evolving from one minute to the next in their growth and development. Toddlers are already going through plenty and to expect them to listen and to conform all the time is just unrealistic. This is partially because in addition to constantly growing, toddlers are constantly learning as well, so it is no wonder he or she can become easily frustrated and throw a fit or have an emotional outburst. The parent at this point should compassionately but purposefully overrule the toddler's choice when this happens.

One instance when a parent should overrule his or her child's behavior is when the child hits or injures him or herself and others. This is an obvious one because when a child hits another child or adult, it is usually a sign that he or she is overwhelmed and needs assistance of some kind from mom, dad or the caretaker. Maybe even offer the toddler something else to hit or kick safely like a pillow; that way the toddler's feelings have a safe outlet to be expressed in a healthy manner without hurting anybody or him or herself. Whatever you do as the parent, it is very crucial to acknowledge the child's emotions and feelings as well, no matter how exaggerated or ridiculous they might seem to you.

Another example of when a parent should

overrule his or her toddler's choices is when he or she has a tantrum. This is necessary to prevent the toddler from inadvertently hurting him or herself or others during the explosion of emotion. One technique is to place the child on something soft like a couch because this will hopefully prevent the child from hurting him or herself during the emotional episode. Maybe even put a few blankets on the floor and let the child have at it. As long as the toddler is safe, let him or her express the strong emotions.

Quick Tip: In order to convince a toddler to stop throwing a fit, perhaps get on the floor yourself and pretend to throw a fit. The toddler will immediately stop doing it out of shock and surprise. Sounds ridiculous, but it works.

Overruling the toddler's choice to repeatedly take away toys from other kids requires an intervention on the parents' part to make the misbehavior stop. This misbehavior often happens because the child is subconsciously asking for a helping hand from his or her caretaker with setting his or her own boundaries with the other kids. Since a two to three-year-old toddler doesn't usually know how to set proper limits and boundaries with his or her peers, this is when mom and dad step in. The parent or caretaker of the toddler could model the behavior he or she wants to see the child enact by sharing the toy between themselves.

There are plenty of instances when mom or dad must intervene on the toddler's behalf, but, as explained above, some of the more common ones are:

- When the child hits
- When the child throws a temper tantrum
- When the child takes away toys from other kids

It can be challenging as a parent or caretaker to handle the fragile balance between boundaries and freedom with your toddler because on the one hand, you want to keep him or her safe while also letting the toddler explore the world around him or her. This freedom is priceless to your toddler, yet your toddler is priceless to you. Therefore, it is important to counterbalance the immeasurable worth of the little one with the value of the toddler's curiosity in learning about the world around him or her. You need to be selective when you choose to intervene because the last thing you want to do is compromise your toddler's well-being and happiness.

The well-being and happiness of your toddler

now and in the future as an adult depends on the parent(s) setting and enforcing reasonable limits and healthy boundaries now. Otherwise the parent or caretaker could risk the child's well-being and health in addition to compromising his or her future because he or she might not understand the cause and effect relationship of choices leading to consequences and of consequences leading to hopefully better choices. This relationship affects everything in the toddler's life from how he or she thinks to how the toddler as an adult lives his or her life in the future. Therefore, don't cheat your child out of a learning opportunity that will positively benefit the child's life in so many ways, like the child as an adult being accountable and responsible for his or her actions. It may be tempting to do this because you don't want to see your child get upset as a result of the enforced consequences, but just remember that emotions are temporary whereas lessons learned last a lifetime.

A growing and evolving toddler becomes a self-governing adult functioning optimally in society because he or she has learned to internalizes and understand the need for limits and boundaries. Without boundaries and limits, people would just do whatever they want whenever they want with no consideration of how that can affect other people and their lives. As a result, society would be chaotic. Functional members of society understand that boundaries keep us safe by defining what is socially acceptable. It is acceptable and possible to interact with people while also respecting their personal space and boundaries.

To explain, boundaries and limits teach children what they can and cannot do regarding their actions and behavior which also shapes their thoughts as well. In other words, the child as an adult will have thoughts and thinking patterns directly tied into not only the limits and boundaries taught but also the emotions tied into how those limits and boundaries were taught. Therefore, if the parents or caretakers carefully employ positive parenting and healthy discipline now, the child will benefit the most now and later in life. This is because as an adult, he or she will not only be able to know right from wrong given cause and effect but also have a strong ability to discern right from wrong in his or her own life.

Chapter Four:
Positive Communication
With Your Child

I t is important to understand what communication is first. It is loosely defined as the exchange or transmission of information. This exchange of information allows human beings to act and react to each other and to the world around them in such a way that people can both discern and interpret the message received and given out as a result. It is this message that determines the next response and message. In fact, communication is almost like a feedback loop of sorts with input, output, actions and reactions.

A crucial part of parenting is communicating with your child in a positive manner, because doing so sets the stage for further positive communication down the road with peers, family and friends. In addition, how parents, other adult figures and even peers in the child's life communicate through words and body language makes a difference because the child is still learning about the world and other people through communication. If people communicate with the child in a happy, optimistic manner, the little one may think the world is a happy, optimistic place. Yet if the child's peers communicate with the child in an impatient, angry manner, the child might think the world is an impatient, angry place. However, positive communication with the child will have a beneficial effect on everything and everybody in the child's world, even as an adult.

Communicating positively with the child must start with the parent or caretaker first, from how he or she frames his or her words to the tone of the parent's voice to even his or her body language when interacting with the child. The child will pick up on the communication signals and cues the parent puts out and projects on a day-to-day basis. In addition, the child will also mirror his or her parent's emotional projections and respond back to the parent with his or her own ways of communicating depending on their stage of development, experience and nurture. If the parent or caretaker nurtures the child with positive communication, the child will be more likely to respond to the parent in a more productive and positive way that will promote the child's well-being and the relationship between both the parent and the child. Communicating in an open, direct and constructive manner brings people closer to understanding one another.

Quick Tip: It is important to remember to communicate with the child at his or her development level to help him or her understand what is being said in contrast to talking to the child at the parent's language skill level.

Tips to Encourage Communication

One action parents can take to communicate more positively is to project a calm demeanor, in part because children not only imitate and replicate what they see and hear but also they may respond to how the parent presents him or herself. For example, if the parent's appearance includes furrowed brows and pursed lips, his or her toddler will be more likely to react to him or her in kind. Yet if the parent's appearance includes a calm and relaxed facial expression and body language, his or her child will be more likely to respond to the parent in an encouraging way to facilitate even more communication. How the parent presents and projects him or herself makes a difference because every interaction parents have with their children sets the tempo for further similar interactions in the family and later in the bigger world.

Another action parents can undertake to communicate more positively with their child is to use and maintain good eye contact. This is helpful for communicating with the child because it not only gets his or her attention but also enhances the special connection between parent and child. Too often parents are looking at their cellphones or computers, so to initiate eye contact is a good way to lessen that distracting preoccupation with electronics. Eye contact is clearly important because looking directly into the child's eyes allows the parent to assess what step or direction to take next in response to his or her little one. This is helpful in parenting because an individual's eyes usually show what he or she is thinking and feeling. Parents can, in turn, use this information to understand the child at that particular moment, especially when he or she is having trouble using words at the earlier stages of development.

Positive communication also includes talking *with* the child in comparison to talking *at* the child. When the parent talks at the child, he or she will be less likely to listen because talking at the child usually results in the child not really receiving the proper attention he or she deserves in the first place. In addition, it would seem to talk at the child is for everybody else's benefit but the child. On the other hand, when the parent talks *with* his or her child, the child is more likely to listen because the communication is more personal and direct as compared to impersonal and indirect. How the parent talks with the child makes a big difference as to how he or she perceives the parent and the world itself, so take care to talk to your child as you would want to be spoken to yourself.

Furthermore, communicating with the child also becomes easier if the parent or caretaker is in close proximity to the child, compared to being halfway across the room, in part because physical closeness relays the message that you are indeed there for the child. If the parent is in close proximity to the toddler, he or she will also be more likely to communicate with the parent. Communicating with the child just doesn't work if the parent is physically far away from his or her little one. In short, it is okay to be physically close to the child while also respecting his or her personal space and boundaries.

In addition to being in close proximity to the

child to improve upon communication, how the parent's physical person is oriented toward the child can also make a difference. This is because although the parent can be in close proximity to the child to have a conversation, the parent turning his or her back to the child will most likely result in a lower quality of interaction between them because the parent is facing *away* from him or her. The last thing the parent wants to do as a parent is to give his or her child the impression the parent is ignoring him or her by turning his or her back to the child. Clearly facing the child when interacting and communicating sends the signal that the parents value their child by giving him or her their undivided attention.

Positive communication also includes communicating at the child's development level. In other words, don't insult the child by talking to him or her as if the child was still a few months old. This won't really help the child's development in any way because the parent is talking below his or her child's level of language skill capabilities. Instead, talk to the child at his or her level, and not the parent's level. It is also advisable to introduce to the child language that is a little above his or her language capabilities while still communicating at mostly the child's level. That way the child might also experience growth in his or her language capabilities allowing for easier communication between parent and child.

An integral part of communicating in a positive manner is listening. Listening is such an obvious part of communication that people often take it for granted. However, listening is just as important as talking when interacting with the child. The problem is people usually listen to answer and not to understand what is being communicated. Clearly, it is important to listen to the child because it helps the child to feel understood and validated.

Positive communication with the child also includes giving him or her a safe outlet to express those feelings because if the parent or caretaker does this, the child will be more likely to talk to the parent whether the child is mad, sad or glad. The parent or caretaker could also engage the child in some kind of sport or other physical activity to express and release his or her feelings as well. It is important to give the child a safe outlet for feelings because this will improve communication between both of you as the child expresses and releases those emotions first. Even adults can sometimes use a safe outlet to express themselves.

Quick Tip: Another outlet for the toddler's strong feelings could be something creative like painting or drawing as it is a form of expression the toddler will be able to take part in. Even finger paints can be therapeutic.

There are many ways for parents to encourage communication that is more positive, and some of those ways are:

- Project calm demeanor
- Use and maintain eye contact
- Talk with the child, and not at the child
- Be in close proximity
- Orient body position towards child
- Communicate at the child's level
- Listen
- Give outlet to express pent-up feelings

More Inside Information on Communicating Positively

When trying to communicate with a toddler, it is vital to ask direct questions because he or she may sometimes easily become frustrated or overwhelmed if the caretaker uses descriptive and detailed language above the child's language development level. It is best to use language that is short, simple and to the point because this is what toddlers best understand. For example, when asking "yes" or "no" questions, stick to the basic sentence structure of subject and verb because it is more clear and concise to a two-to-three-year-old child via something like "car go fast." In short, the parent or caretaker will improve communicative interactions between him or herself and the child by using frank and candid language that directly addresses the issue.

Communicating with the child in a positive manner also includes getting down to his or her eye-level, so that the parent doesn't seem so imposing with a bigger silhouette than the child. For example, when I met Goofy at Disneyland, I was about four years old. I got so frightened from Goofy's towering height over mine, that I ran and hid behind my mother's legs in direct response to the situation. Likewise, getting down to the child's eye level will make the parent appear more friendly and available to that specific child. This will definitely improve the positive communication between parent and child.

Positive communication with the child also depends upon the tone of the parent's or caretaker's voice. For example, if the parent inflects his or her voice to sound harsh and firm when communicating with the toddler, the child will be more likely to react instead of thinking about what the parent is trying to say to him or her. On the other hand, if the parent inflects his or her voice to sound more even and calm, the child will be more likely to consider what is being said. Clearly, this improves the interaction between parent and child.

Making time to talk with the child is very important! Otherwise, the child may feel disregarded or even neglected to some degree if the parent doesn't make the time to interact with him or her daily. Even if it is just for ten minutes at the end of the day, the child will feel more loved and validated if the parent or caretaker makes time to communicate and interact with him or her. This is because mom's and dad's attention is priceless to a young child.

One way to make time to interact with the child is to engage in age-appropriate conversation during everyday tasks. Perhaps while picking up toys together, or you could weave a conversation in while reading a story together. No matter what the parent does to communicate, it is important to make the time for that communication first.

Actively listening to the child is also of great value because it shows the child that the parent or caretaker is more interested in what he or she has to say, in comparison to just hearing them, where the adult doesn't really listen to understand the message of the speaker. The parent should use body language as well as words to communicate to the child in order to show that he or she is actively listening. For example, perhaps the parent could gesture with his or her head to show he or she is actively listening by nodding up and down in assent as the child talks with his or her parent. The parent could also verbally agree with words such as yes to encourage the child to talk with him or her, and repeat back what the child has said, e.g. "the car is your favorite toy?".

Another reason reading books to the child is that it is another way to communicate with him or her because the parent or caretaker not only spends time with the child, but the parent can also positively express words to his or her child as the parent reads to them. This is most definitely positive communication with the growing toddler because it will also increase his or her language capabilities with new vocabulary, thus allowing for more communication between parent and child. Try to read books to the child daily as this will increase the bonding time in which the parent connects with him or her. This will also increase the child's likelihood of responding to the age-appropriate books read to him or her, especially if there are pictures in the book of everyday items the child recognizes from his or her own daily routine.

Additionally, the parent could even play with his or her toddler by playing with some of the same toys in the same way as the toddler. For example, dad could play with the model trains with his son by pushing them along the toy train-tracks and expressing "choo choo" like his or her toddler. Try to let the child lead the play session while mom or dad follows along. In addition, it is also good to play a little bit with the toddler every day to encourage the child's imagination and development in so many areas. In fact, it would seem the creative art of play is beneficial for everyone involved, especially the toddler, because it demonstrates to the toddler various things like how to take turns and how to win or lose. These lessons will carry over into the adult life of the toddler as well.

As mentioned earlier in the book, when communicating with the toddler, it is important to use positive language. Remember that words such as "no" or "don't" should be avoided unless the parent or caretaker really needs to use them for an emergency like the child running into the street all of a sudden. Instead, change the focus a little and try to paraphrase and emphasize the action the parent wants the child to accomplish. In addition, try to exclude words that shame, name-call or ridicule the child because this will only lead to the child shutting down on the parent due to the child feeling belittled and less than. On the other hand, compassionate words produce positive and happy toddlers that want to interact and communicate more with the world around them. Positive communication is clearly an important part of the child's growth and development because it motivates him or her to interact with other people and to discover the bigger world beyond mom and dad.

There are many methods for improving communication with your child, including:

- Be direct
- Get down to child's eye level
- Watch tone of voice
- Make time to talk
- Actively listen
- Read books
- Use positive language

Positive communication with the child clearly requires the parent or caretaker to be more sensitive to and cognizant of the child's needs. It also requires the parent to consider that his or her child is an individual in his or her own right with growing language capabilities and needs exclusive to the child's age, development level, experiences, nurture and more. When people say children are a product of their environment, they are onto something because children internalize and emulate what they observe their parents and caretakers doing and communicating from day to day. If mom and dad are positive on a daily basis, their child will also be more upbeat and positive as well, whether that be now or in the future. It is important to remember that your little one looks up to you for guidance and structure with communication in a positive way.

Chapter Five:
Positive Parenting And Discipline Action Plan For Toddlers

Positive parenting and discipline go hand-in-hand because both work together to give the child the best life possible through structure, guidance and teaching the child with love no matter what. They are intricately connected because positive parenting needs healthy discipline to be successful and discipline isn't as effective without unconditional love. In addition, positive parenting and healthy discipline give both the parent and the child a healthy balance to coexist in because both are respected, understood and highly-esteemed in the process. Therefore, it would seem positive parenting and discipline are quite interdependent.

Be that as it may, positive parenting and discipline don't always go as smoothly as parents would like sometimes, especially when parents try to introduce something new to the child like a new limit. It is then when parents should try their best to be patient with the child and the process. However, all parents have their breaking point when they react and respond to the situation instead of acting and thinking about what is best for the child. This is when parents must up their game as parents to manage the situation as best as they can without compromising the child or themselves. It is important after a difficulty to restore a sense of normalcy for both the child and the parent in order for both to communicate and interact in a healthy manner again.

Quick Tip: It is okay for mom, dad, or the caretaker to take a time-out to gather, center, and compose him or herself before returning to the awesome job of parenting! Take a breather if too tipped over emotionally.

Skills to Minimize Arguments and Yelling

In order for positive parenting and discipline to work, parents must sometimes pay attention to what they can control in comparison to what they cannot when it comes to attempting to parent the child the best they can given the situation and their parenting abilities. The parent cannot control the child's reaction to the new limit, but the parent can control his or her response to the child's reaction to the new limit. The last thing the parents want to do as a parent is lose his or her cool because the toddler will then see he or she can push the parents' buttons with his or her emotional reaction(s). It is important to remember as the parent that the parent has the power and authority to guide and discipline the toddler in a healthy and optimistic manner. This is a great responsibility and must be handled with the utmost care, love and consideration for the toddler.

However, sometimes a toddler likes to argue with his or her parent(s) about the new limit that is set for him or her because the toddler is upset over not having control over his or her own life and choices. Yet the toddler is not always able to make his or her own choices given age and things like development stage. In addition, when the toddler throws a fit or gets upset over a new limit imposed, it is easy to become frustrated with the situation. This is when the parent must disengage from the situation in order to remain calm and composed enough to act and think what would be the best thing for the toddler right now.

Even if the toddler argues with the parent, don't argue back. Arguing with a toddler usually doesn't achieve much anyway. Being argumentative for the toddler gives him or her an opportunity to try to regain some autonomy and control back. The toddler might even amp up his or her game to see how the parent reacts if pushed by the arguing. Although it might be tempting to argue back with a three-year-old child, it is highly recommended to not give in because then the toddler has accomplished something known as the extinction curve.

The extinction curve is defined as when a specific action stops in response to another action, like a parent acquiescing to the initial demand or request from his or her toddler's begging and whining. The more the toddler complains, the more the toddler hopes his or her parent will give in. If the parent does acquiesce, then the toddler has achieved the extinction of the parent's limit(s) or rule(s). On the other hand, if the parent repeatedly disengages from the toddler's whining or complaining, the little one will eventually learn mom and dad aren't going to give in. As a result, the toddler stops his or her complaining, thus leading to an extinction of the initial behavior. In short, the extinction curve also works in the favor of the parent(s) as well.

Once the initial behavior of whining, complaining or throwing a fit has stopped, it is also important for the parent to agree with the

toddler on something in contrast to disagreeing when arguing. For example, the parent could agree with the toddler on how he or she feels in response to the new limit implemented and show empathy to his or her toddler. This agreement on something the toddler understands and values also has the effect of extinguishing the toddler's whiny behavior as well. This is because the toddler will see that mom, dad or the caretaker understands where the little one is coming from regarding the situation of being vulnerable and defenseless as a three-year-old child. Agreement instead of argument is clearly more effective at helping the caretaker to positively parent with healthy discipline out of love no matter what.

However, parenting and disciplining can be challenging when your little one doesn't want to listen. Toddlers can argue until they are blue in the face to state their case. Sometimes the arguing can even lead to yelling. One reason this may be is because toddlers' prefrontal cortex isn't fully developed quite yet, which means a toddler's skill at emotional regulation isn't all there yet. This may lead to emotional meltdowns when the toddler becomes overwhelmed and frustrated. Similarly, when both child and parent yell, it is because there is some kind of skill lacking. In fact, the biggest reason new parents yell is that they lack the skills to positively parent and discipline the toddler. In short, yelling is easier but a much less effective way to convince the toddler to acquiesce.

Yelling also occurs because we are selfish sometimes. In short, the parent wants to insist on having his or her way without really considering what is best for the toddler's well-being. The question is if the parent is yelling or admonishing the toddler because he or she is personally irritated with the toddler or if the parent is trying to look out for the toddler and his or her well-being. And although it is less difficult to shout and yell, it is more damaging to the toddler because he or she will most definitely mirror his or her caretaker's behavior as a result. The parent needs to find a more effective way to take care of and to educate the toddler.

Clearly, minimizing arguing and yelling between a parent and a child requires some skill, and some of those skills are:

- Pay attention to what you can control
- Disengage
- Don't argue back
- Use the extinction curve to diminish arguing
- Agree with toddler after an argument
- Don't yell to begin with
- Be cognizant of selfish motives for yelling

Positive parenting and discipline become difficult when the parent focuses so much on being upset that he or she becomes preoccupied with those strong feelings resulting in them forgetting their role in the child's life. This obviously isn't good because then the child can usurp the parent if the parent is experiencing an identity dilemma by forgetting his or her role in the child's life. This role reversal of sorts would be damaging to the toddler, especially if it ends up culminating in the toddler parenting the parent. Dysfunction would overtake the toddler's life and home, and this is not what parenting is about. Parenting is about loving and raising a healthy, functional human being capable of governing him or herself someday, and not the other way around.

The parent in the previous case needs to consciously make a decision to parent and nurture the child and then question how he or she is going to engage in being a positive parent without losing his or her cool all the time. In fact, it would seem positive parenting is more than a conscious decision, it is a way of life for both the parent(s) and the child. Clearly, this way of life is healthier because thinking skillfully and consciously taking action in comparison to just reacting and responding emotionally to the situation is clearly good for all parties involved.

Detailed Plan of Action for Changing Behavior

It is also good for the parent to know that the toddler understands and assimilates more than he or she can express and vocalize at this age given development stage or phase. This is the reason why it is important to focus on explaining what is in the present and what could be in the immediate future. This way the toddler understands better what is happening and what needs to happen to hopefully modify the behavior and correct the situation to something more optimal for the toddler's life. All it takes is a little finesse at language to go into explanation with your little one.

The next step to take after detailing and explaining the present and the immediate future to the toddler is to practice what has just been preached. In other words, the toddler needs you to model the behavior you want from him or her. Maybe even role-play the new standard of behavior to get the point across to the toddler. In other words, words are a start but then take action to change the behavior of the toddler, instead of focusing on the incorrect behavior. Another important thing to consider is that every toddler has a different learning style and curve when you teach him or her the new standard of behavior.

Quick Tip: Perhaps try role-reversal with the toddler to get the point across when teaching a new behavior. This will help the toddler to better understand the need for the new behavior, as the parent plays the child and the child pretends to be mommy or daddy.

Yet in order for this to happen, the toddler has to calm down first, especially if he or she was throwing a fit or yelling at mom. One good idea to get the toddler to calm down is to assign him or her a place to relax, like sitting on the couch for a few minutes, away from other children or other distractions. Once the toddler has calmed down, then it is okay to teach him or her the new standard of behavior. Even adults have a hard time focusing when they are upset.

Be that as it may, it is important for the adult in the parent-child relationship to teach his or her toddler a few steps to be successful in learning a new behavior. Those steps include:

- The toddler learning how to follow instructions from the caretaker

- Teaching the toddler to receive no for an answer plus critiques of behavior

- Teaching the toddler to receive the consequences

The first step is to learn how to follow instructions from mom or dad. Maybe mom or dad could model the new behavior to show the toddler what it is at first so the toddler understands the acton required instead of just talking about it. Besides, toddlers carefully watch what you do in comparison to what you say as the parent.

The second step is to teach the toddler to receive "no" for an answer a well critiques of the initial misbehavior. This could be done by the parent using the word "no" intermittently with an action to get the point across so the toddler gets used to the word and what it means. It would seem "no" is best understood by using both words and action to describe it on a level the toddler can understand. In addition to the word "no", the toddler will need to become accustomed to receiving mom's and dad's critiques of his or her initial behavior. In order to train the child to do this, perhaps critique something less serious than a teachable discipline moment, so the child becomes used to it. For example, if you and your child are out walking and you see litter on the ground, you could say, "that is naughty. It makes me sad." Then when you use that phrase for a behavior of your child, he or she will have some understanding of what you mean.

The third step is to receive the consequence for the misbehavior. Mom or dad should dole out the consequences sooner than later to instill in the toddler an understanding of the cause and effect of the consequence. If mom or dad waits to enact the consequence, the toddler will miss out on a learning opportunity if too much time passes between setting a limit and enforcing it through consequences, because the child will simply have forgotten what they've done.

Lastly, the fourth step if necessary is to teach the toddler how to disagree appropriately if the toddler doesn't agree with mom or dad regarding the discipline actions just described. In other words, it is okay to disagree, as long as there are guidelines for doing so. Clearly, acquiring a new behavior is a learning process, especially for the toddler. The goal here is to teach autonomy through cause and effect relationships one lesson at a time.

Changing a toddler's behavior takes some work on the parent's or caretaker's part, but to make it easier, here is a summarized plan of action to make it happen:

- Describe present behavior and possible future behaviors.
- Practice new behaviors immediately
- Teach toddler to follow instructions
- Teach toddler to accept "no" answers and critiques of behavior
- Have toddler receive consequences
- Disagree appropriately

Another goal and action plan for positive parenting and discipline is to teach the toddler to stop hitting. This type of behavior is typical and common for toddlers because they don't have the emotional regulation skills at that age to self-govern the way adults can with their feelings and emotions. Instead, toddlers easily become inundated by their strong feelings and act out from time to time. Yet this behavior of acting out and hitting must stop because it only causes pain to the receiving party and eventually to the toddler whether in the present or later in life as an adult. In short, although hitting is typical behavior for toddlers, it isn't right for them to engage in it.

What is appropriate to remember in relation to hitting is that your toddler will often undergo development stages in which a milestone is eventually reached by him or her. A milestone is an event marking a significant change in development for the toddler. Typically, when a milestone is about to happen, the toddler can become a little more irritable and cranky resulting in more acting out with belligerent behavior. This is common because many changes are taking place and the toddler's ever-growing brain can barely keep up with them. In short, toddlers don't possess the developmental skills necessary to handle all this. Instead, they suddenly become more delicate and tender in their emotional state when they are stressed. This is true for adults too. Yet this is a normal process of development requiring a lot of assistance from the mom, dad or the caretaker.

However, the caretaker of the child needs to take

care of him or herself first, before even thinking about helping the toddler because otherwise chaos results when mom or dad ignores his or her self-care. As a result of mom or dad's welfare being compromised due to lack of self-care, the toddler will also suffer less than optimal care from mom or dad. This can easily happen because the parent's inclination is to love the child first. It is easy to forget to take care of ourselves. Yet if parents forget this simple rule, they will be less effective as parents and as people in general. Nothing is accomplished by ignoring self-care.

If parents can take care of themselves better, they will be more effective as parents because they will be able to help people in general in addition to their young offspring. For example, the parent can keep track of his or her behavior and feelings in response to the toddler hitting, because parents do have responsive reactions and emotions too. Yet if the caretaker can avoid being carried away by his or her emotions, the toddler will clearly benefit from his or her mom or dad thinking and taking action as compared to instinctively reacting and responding without careful thought.

Steps to Stop the Toddler from Hitting

In other words, sometimes mom or dad needs a minute to calm down as well. One suggestion to do this via self-care is to engage in something that brings you peace of mind. This could be anything from a hot bubble bath or a walk on a nature trail somewhere. As a result, you will be more centered and calm as a person. The toddler will notice your projection of this and in turn, be calmer as well, instead of hitting another individual. Taking care of yourself first is vital, in part because toddlers mirror what mom and dad do in comparison to what they say. In addition, hopefully, mom or dad taking a time-out will result in him or her being more cognizant of doing what is right by the child, in contrast to just effecting what is momentarily convenient for the parent. I will go into more detail about self-care in Chapter Seven.

The second step to take regarding the toddler hitting is to set a simple but firm limit with him or her in the moment while the toddler is doing the deed. Something like, "you can't hit other children," is direct and to the point with a three-year-old child. In addition, if you must, physically remove the toddler from the situation as well. This way, the toddler will learn that every time he or she hits, no more playing with other children will be allowed as a result. Parents have to be firm to get the behavior to stop sooner than later.

The third step to convincing the toddler to stop

hitting is to present him or her with a centered and calm adult to interact with, in comparison to an upset parent as a result of the interaction. If the toddler observes his or her caretaker as centered and calm, the toddler will hopefully mirror and model the behavior him or herself too. Clearly, it is important to be an example for your toddler because he or she will assimilate what the parent projects and in turn, project it him or herself through a process known as conditioning. Hopefully, with enough time and practice, the toddler will be able to begin to govern him or herself a little better.

The fourth step to take regarding the toddler hitting is to connect with your toddler. Find out why he or she is acting out and hitting, to begin with. In addition, remember that a three-year-old child's reason for hitting may not be as sound as an adult's logic and reasoning, and that's okay. Perhaps the child is hitting because he or she is trying to fulfill some need not currently being met. Whatever the case may be, it is important to be aware of this need because then the parent can employ empathy to connect with his or her little one regarding that need.

The fifth and final step to persuading the toddler not to hit is to address his or her approach to fulfill the unmet need. It is important to address the toddler's approach of hitting if the behavior is to change presently. Perhaps suggest to the little one some strategies that are more suitable and effectual than hitting another individual, whether a child or even the caretaker. Once some strategies are identified, perhaps mom or dad could again model the newer approach to fulfilling the toddler's unmet need.

Stopping a toddler from hitting requires mom or dad to:

- Be calmer via self-care
- Set simple but firm limit
- Present toddler with a centered and calm adult to interact with afterwards
- Connect with him or her via empathy
- Address toddler's approach to fulfilling unmet need

Tips to Convince Toddler to Listen the First Time

Besides arguing, yelling and hitting, it is also important to convince the child to listen the first time when setting a limit in order to positively parent and discipline said toddler. The first step to getting the toddler to listen and behave on the first request is learning to think like a toddler. This is invaluable because it is kind of a role-reversal that can give the parent some insight into the situation of what his or her child may think, feel, and believe regarding limits, discipline and boundaries. It may help the parent to understand a toddler's reasoning process of why versus why not, too. In fact, why would a toddler deliberately choose to do something not fun as per the parent's request? They wouldn't. Yet once the parent understands the toddler's thinking process by getting to know his or her toddler better through playing, conversing, and just hanging out, the parent can ultimately sway the child to listen the first time. In short, the approach is everything with getting a toddler to listen the first time.

Quick Tip: It may sound silly, but acting like the toddler will often get him or her to stop long enough to pay attention to the parent when you want the child to listen to the caretaker.

The second step to getting a child to listen is to control your emotions regarding the situation, because otherwise if you are explosive in yelling at the toddler, they will be less likely to acquiesce to your requests anyway. On the other hand, if you are calm with your tone of voice, facial expressions and posture, the child will be more likely to abide by the rule you just set. After all, the parent is the one with power and control.

The third step to convincing a child to listen is to pair the consequences with the communication. For example, if the parent changes his or her tone of voice to a louder one, the child knows the consequence will be more severe. In addition, if the parent does this enough, the toddler will eventually learn to listen without the consequence given the parent's conditioning of his response to it.

The fourth step to get the child to listen is to

change your words from static into something invaluable like gold. This means toddlers will be more likely to listen to the parent if he or she follows through on what is said. Otherwise, words have no meaning and are indeed worthless to the toddler. If the parent wants his or her word to be golden, then the parent needs to definitely implement consequences which are tied to the communication.

The fifth step to swaying a child to listen is to work on the relationship between the child and the parent, in part because the parent's job is to love the child no matter what and even if. If the child is aware that somebody special loves them, then he or she will be more likely to listen, given that the child wants that love and attention. In short, the child will listen for want of mom's and dad's love and attention.

There are many ways to convince a toddler to

listen, with some of the more pertinent ways being:

- Think like a toddler
- Control your emotions
- Pair consequence with communication
- Change words from trash to gold
- Work on parent-child relationship

Sleeping Advice for Toddlers

Another goal in positively parenting and disciplining the toddler is to get the child to fall asleep when needed. This can be a challenge for most parents because they cannot control such things as whether or not the child will sleep. The last thing a parent wants is to be upset because of the child's outright refusal of things like bedtime. However, what the parent can do to convince the child to do things like fall asleep is to pick his or her battles wisely through choosing issues the parent(s) can control, like the choices given to the child when enforcing the rule or limit concerning bedtime. For example, a parent cannot control when his or her child sleeps, but he or she can control things like if the child is quiet, the bedroom door can be left open to allow for light in the room.

Behavior of the toddler can be gently persuaded by agreeable routines for things like bedtime. Such routines set the stage for the toddler's behavior because they promote good health and therefore, good brain development. Give the toddler something to look forward to at bedtime, like spending time with mom and dad, having a story read to them, a hug. Be that as it may, if the toddler doesn't like the routine, he or she might test you by throwing a tantrum. They do this by something known as the intermittent reinforcement schedule. If the parent responds and reacts randomly to the toddler's pushing and complaining, then the toddler has indeed won the control battle by reinforcing mom's behavior through his own behavior. However, if mom or dad just doesn't respond, but instead walks away for a moment, perhaps the toddler will realize what once worked with his or her caretakers no longer works. Then the control battle is won.

Convincing the child to fall asleep is easier if mom or dad:

- Avoids control battles
- Wins control battles if they can't be avoided
- Picks battles wisely
- Has a routine for bedtime

Helping the Toddler Gain More Confidence

Positive parenting and disciplining the toddler actually helps him or her to gain some confidence through learning and mastering tasks appropriate for his or her age and development level. In short, the process for a toddler to gain confidence in him or herself has four necessary steps. The first step is to give the toddler a task you think he or she can handle. This is important because it says to the toddler that you as the parent has confidence in his or her capabilities to accomplish something. This is big to the toddler.

Yet in the same token the parent hopes his or her

toddler actually fails at the task. This is because then the toddler will learn something valuable like persistence and determination in trying again. This second step of the child failing at a task teaches so many things, especially what not to do. In fact, it seems people learn the most from what they have failed in comparison to what they have accomplished. Mistakes teach more than perfection anyway.

The third step in teaching confidence to a toddler is to let the consequences for the mistake teach the child not to do it again. Age-appropriate consequences are a very valuable teaching aid because they can determine the toddler's behavior time and again through taking responsibility for his or her actions. However, it is also invaluable to have empathy for the toddler when they are feeling the effects of their mistakes.

The fourth and final step to helping your toddler gain confidence is to give him or her the same challenge again in the hopes of eventual success. If the toddler has learned anything at this point, it is that repetition is an effective teacher as well. Hopefully, the toddler will succeed this time as he or she struggles to achieve said task. In fact, it would seem that repeating one's mistakes is very effective for schooling anybody at any age.

Clearly, mom or dad can help the toddler gain confidence in many ways, but some of the more important methods include:

- Give toddler task he or she can handle
- Hope toddler fails at task
- Let consequences teach
- Give same challenge/task again

Clearly, action plans are necessary to teach, provide structure for and guide toddlers with positive parenting and discipline with unconditional love no matter what and even if. It is important for the parent to wholeheartedly engage in these positive parenting and discipline techniques for the sake of the child because the eventual goal for the child someday is to learn how to govern him or herself as a stable, healthy adult even if human beings don't come with a set of instructions.

Chapter Six:
Common Discipline
Mistakes

C ommon discipline mistakes means learning is taking place with the parent trying to structure, guide and teach the child with unconditional love no matter what and even if, in comparison to being unsuccessful as a parent. We all need to learn sometime. Similar to a toddler learning through failing at a task, sometimes the best way for a parent to learn is to also fail at a task the first few times. As I have explained, people learn best through their mistakes, especially with positive parenting and disciplining the little one. Learning is a process, and with children, it becomes a trial and error process as parents try new techniques to figure out what works best regarding the discipline of his or her toddler.

Toddlers can be challenging to positively parent and discipline for many reasons. One reason is that every toddler is uniquely different regarding discipline and stage of development. In addition, the parent(s) should also consider the toddler's nature and genetics, nurture, e.g. home environment and experience given daily events or occurrences in the toddler's life. It can also be hard to change our parenting style from what we learned from our own parents to something new and different. All these aspects must be considered before embarking on the journey of parenting and discipline.

Discipline mistakes are very common because parents are human. Humans by nature are fallible and human nature itself is not as straightforward as a set of instructions to guide that nature. Be that as it may, human nature can be conditioned through repetitive experiences leading to a change in outlook, attitude or behavior. It is this change in behavior that will tell a parent if what he or she is doing to discipline the child is working for that specific child. Even more challenging is the fact that toddlers have a steep learning curve because they are still developing and growing. However, children are like sponges; they soak up everything they see and hear in their environment.

In addition, children internalize what they are taught by the means of discipline which sometimes leads to their emotional expression of that limit, rule or boundary. In other words, toddlers also teach their parents as well through their responsive reactions and actions as they are guided and taught through positive parenting and unconditional love. However, the adult in the relationship needs to be willing to be the teacher and the student sometimes, letting the child take the lead as he or she teaches us what works and doesn't work regarding discipline from mom and dad. Nevertheless, parents must instill values through discipline lessons and experiences that last a lifetime through their example, as the child often is a reflection of his or her parents.

Ten Discipline Mistakes Parents Typically Make

Sometimes parents can have unrealistic expectations of their child's abilities for many reasons. One of them is a lack of information on the toddler's phase of development and the resulting capabilities. In short, parents aren't aware of what their little one is capable of at a given age unless they seek out information about it or unless the parents have had previous experience taking care of and raising children. Even then, some parents don't quite understand that children are not little adults and shouldn't be treated as such. Children need to have a childhood too and expecting them to perform at a level way above their development phase and capabilities is just unrealistic and impractical.

Another common discipline mistake, in addition to expecting children to act older than they are is catering to children. Understandably, parents want their children to have the best life possible. Yet catering to their every whim is not a feasible reality either because then the child, as a result, may end up becoming spoiled and expect people in the future to also cater to him or her even as an adult. That isn't realistic nor healthy. It is healthy, however, to indulge the toddler every once in a while for a job well done but it is not healthy to overindulge them for every small victory. In addition, the toddler may become lazy and inert if the parent coddles him or her every second. This might result in the child not being able to think and act for him or herself when a need or want materializes. The last thing a parent wants for his or her child is to become so accustomed to being spoon-fed that he or she can't do it him or herself.

What can be done to avoid the next discipline mistake is to follow through on consequences. In other words, sometimes parents do not follow through on action once the words are spoken whether it be promises or consequences. This is not good for the child. If a parent doesn't routinely follow through with action after the words are spoken, the toddler might just take the parent less seriously. As a result, the toddler might ignore and not listen to the parent when an imminent threat is pending. On the other hand, the toddler will take the parent more seriously if he or she follows through once the words are spoken, regardless of the reason for them. A parent with all words and no action is not much of a parenting plan, as there needs to be a balance between the two. In short, too much or too little action and words is not a good thing for the little one.

Babying the child too much is also disadvantageous because the child will come to expect being coddled all the time by mom or dad, even when the child's peer group is not babied twenty-four-seven. This might result in less development growth because the child will respond to the babying and not to his or her development stage instead like his or her peers. If a toddler is constantly babied, he or she will be less likely to fend for him or herself too, if and when the need arises. In addition, a toddler being babied pretty much encourages the child to overly depend on his or her caretakers instead of the toddler working it out for him or herself. Some babying is okay, but too much past the point of the child actually being a baby doesn't really help him or her develop correctly or fully. In short, the child becomes less self-reliant and even more dependent on his or her caretaker(s), thus making the child kind of defenseless. Another way to put it is that the toddler will have less agency and autonomy as a result.

Another common discipline mistake is when the toddler's caretaker(s) neglect to teach the child manners. Some parents even think it is cute when their child acts without manners, e.g. picking his or her nose or physically grabbing toys from other children, excusing it as "children just being children". However, if the toddler doesn't learn to acquire some sense of manners, the child might not be socially accepted as much by his or her peers or other adults that also need to guide and teach the child later in life like his or her teachers. This could be damaging to the toddler, especially when he or she needs to socialize with other toddlers and role models. Yet there is a fine line between teaching manners and forcing them on the child through a strict etiquette discipline session. If the child is too polite and respectful of everybody he or she comes into contact with, perhaps the teaching the child manners becomes something akin to discipline that's too strict for the child's age and development stage. Manners are important but not everything, especially to a three-year-old child.

Quick Tip: If the parent is going to teach the child manners, make sure it is consistent and that everybody is on the same page, otherwise the child could easily get confused with mixed messages from other adults and children regarding manners.

Encouraging poor behavior is also a discipline mistake because children can carry these poor behaviors into adulthood. As a result, they might become a misfit or rebel of sorts later as an adult and get into trouble which, of course, is not good. Encouraging poor behavior in a toddler is like training them to be bad on purpose. Why would a parent do that? Makes no sense, but some parents actually do this because they think it is "cute". However, there is nothing cute about your toddler later in life as an adult being arrested for poor behavior. What a parent thinks is cute or cool now might turn into something worse later in life like drug abuse or violence. In short, encouraging poor behavior is a slippery slope that leads to nowhere but down, and doing so is also psychologically damaging to your offspring. The toddler will get the wrong kind of attention from it as well.

Parents relying on social media to calm and entertain the child is also a discipline blunder but many parents do it because it is convenient and easy. As a result, the child will become too dependent on it and on other things later in life in an attempt to pacify him or herself when the child is upset or just bored. The toddler needs to eventually learn to entertain or occupy him or herself in other healthier activities like playing with blocks or learning the ABCs. Too much screen time is not a good thing because the child could also get physical symptoms from it like headaches from being online too long. The child also becomes more self-involved and less sociable while he or she is staring at mom or dad's new tablet for hours on end. Some screen time is okay, but too much negatively affects the child in more ways than one. The toddler also becomes less active as a result. When my son was little, I had to tell him to get off the computer and to actually go outside and play with his friends.

Another common discipline mistake is not parenting in public for whatever reason. Perhaps mom, dad or the caretaker is too worried about what other people will think. The parent could be shy or he or she might embarrass easily if the child doesn't listen and acts out of bounds. Yet the parent must weigh what is more important at that moment of positive parenting and disciplining. Saving oneself from embarrassment or the child. The answer is obviously the child, and sometimes parenting and discipline have to be done in the moment to avoid something even worse like the child getting hurt from not listening. It is okay to discipline your toddler if he or she needs it to avoid something worse like stepping in front of a moving car.

Quick Tips: In order to get over the fear of public parenting, perhaps take a parenting class with other parents to gain confidence in yourself when parenting in public.

Another unwise parenting move is belittling the child, for the reason that he or she might end up with lower self-esteem and confidence as a result. In addition, the toddler might feel less capable in his or her abilities as an individual and to please mom or dad when a new task materializes. Then the child just stops trying to win his or her caretaker over. This is not a good thing. In other words, it is psychologically and emotionally damaging for mom or dad to belittle their child because the child suffers as a result, especially if the belittling occurs in front of others the child looks up to. In addition to the child's feelings being hurt, he or she will feel less validated and valued. Then the toddler as an adult might look to other individuals more untoward to structure and guide his or her life and end up running with the wrong crowd. Belittling the toddler does nothing for him or her.

Being too rigid with parenting and discipline is not a positive thing for the toddler either. This is because the toddler might feel he or she doesn't have any wiggle room to just be a kid as a result of the strict authoritarian style of parenting. Parenting is not about commanding the child to do something, it is about unconditional love no matter what. Parenting is also not about controlling the child due to the fear he or she will make a mistake, it is about allowing the toddler to make mistakes because that is how he or she will learn something new. Another way of putting it is that toddlers are too young to undergo bootcamp, so don't be a drill sergeant with them. If the toddler has too strict of a home environment, the toddler as an adult might end up repeating history and being too strict and rigid with his or her own kids.

Discipline mistakes are more common than you think, and the most typical ones include:

- Having unrealistic expectations
- Expecting children to act older than what they are
- Not following through on consequences
- Babying the child

- Neglecting to teach the child manners
- Encouraging poor behavior
- Relying on social media too much
- Not parenting in public
- Belittling the child
- Being too rigid

The Inside Scoop on More Common Discipline Mistakes

It is also easy for parents to misunderstand the purpose of discipline. Discipline is not about controlling the child for the sake of the parent's convenience and peace of mind, it is about the child learning and understanding the reasons for and consequences of his or her behaviors and actions. It is about teaching the child how and why to act and behave. Otherwise, the toddler might end up later as an adult associating with more people who don't abide by the limits, rules and boundaries set for them by authority figures such as judges, police and doctors. Discipline is about training human beings to abide by a code of behavior that is acceptable to others and society. It is also about the child learning right from wrong because otherwise, the child will possibly end up getting into serious trouble as an adult. Healthy discipline teaches values through unconditional love no matter what and even if.

Another common discipline mistake is when parents and caretakers alike overreact to every little thing the child or toddler does. It is important not to acknowledge every single infraction because the child might become so scared of the parent's reaction that he or she is afraid to act either way. In addition, unless the parents want to spend all day fighting with their child, it's best to let minor acts of misconduct - such as leaving a single toy on the floor after tidying up - go. Overreacting to the toddler's disobedience is not okay because every time mom or dad yells or freaks out, the poor child will be traumatized with too much drama from his or her parents. Therefore, parents should try to think, act and respond in a healthy way to the toddler's misconduct instead of overreacting like some helicopter parent that watches everything the child does. In addition, the toddler might just tune the parent and his or her overreactions out after a while and ignore them. This could be dangerous because if the child is about to get hurt somehow by touching a hot pan, he or she will be less likely to listen to mom or dad when they do react to the situation with good reason and judgment.

Lack of explanation is also a common discipline blunder because if the child does not understand why they are being chastised or corrected by mom or dad in the first place, he or she will be less likely to listen to the parent or obey him or her when it counts. The toddler not understanding the reasons to act differently than how he or she does naturally means the toddler is more likely to repeat the misbehavior through no fault of his or her own and get in trouble anyway for it. It is important to give the toddler good reasons as to why he or she should act differently. In fact, it may even help to think like a child in order to give him or her a valid reason in the toddler's mind as to why he or she should listen to the parent to begin with. In short, thinking like a child will help the parent to understand his or her child in order to give the toddler a valid reason to behave well.

Overusing punishment is also a bad idea for positive parenting and healthy discipline because the child will only be *controlled* by the punishment instead of *learning* from it. Overusing punishment also traumatizes the child though fear and shock and detracts from his or her childhood because most of it will be spent in his or her room with no television. The toddler might even end up frightened and wary of his or her caretaker because punishment is overused for every little thing like forgetting to pick up just one toy. It is important for parents to be more selective when enforcing positive and negative reinforcement and punishment because otherwise the child will get so used to punishment that he or she will think it's a way of life. This is not good nor healthy for the toddler.

Empty threats, as previously said, are also a less than optimal form of parenting because the toddler will be less likely to take the parent at his or her word when the parent threatens an impending punishment for misbehaving. In addition, if the parent continues to make empty threats, his or her toddler will eventually think the parent is all talk and no action. Empty threats get the parent or caretaker nowhere fast and the toddler just does what he or she wants anyway. This could be bad later in the toddler's life when he or she is an adult because he or she will think most people make empty threats as well. Yet I don't know too many doctors or police officers who make empty threats when it is done for health and safety reasons. In other words, the last thing a toddler needs is for his or her parent to make empty threats because he or she might think the parent and other authority figures are full of hot air.

Nagging is also a common discipline mistake because too much of it can cause the child to isolate him or herself from the parent or caretaker because the toddler doesn't want to constantly hear it. In addition, too much nagging starts to sound like a broken tape recorder because the child will just tune the parent out after a while. It is not okay to harass your own child every second of the day about inconsequential things that won't matter next week. Parents, don't henpeck or bully your own child into submission. The child will feel like he or she isn't capable and this isn't good because toddlers need autonomy and agency to eventually be individuals in their own right separate from their parent(s). In other words, nagging or persistent fault-finding is not good for anybody at any age.

Another common mistake when it comes to discipline is misusing time-outs. Time-outs are meant to be used as a breather for the child when he or she is really upset about something and needs space and time from the situation to calm down. In fact, parents sometimes need time-outs from their child, too. In any case, time-outs should only be for a few minutes and the toddler should never be sent to his or her room to be alone for a time-out. This is because the toddler might just act on his or her strong residual feelings from the situation that got him or her upset in the first place. This could lead to a dangerous situation for the toddler. If the parent gives the toddler a time-out, it should be in his or her parent's presence in the same room or vicinity. Furthermore, time-outs aren't really meant to be used as a punishment, but more as a break for the child when needed.

Quick Tip: Perhaps have the child count to ten if possible or have him or her sing the ABC song to calm down during a time-out.

Bribery is also a common discipline blunder that parents typically make when they want his or her toddler to behave, especially in a public setting like a grocery store or church. For example, mom or dad will give in to the child's whining and crying, and they will end up giving the toddler a toy or some sweet treat to get him or her to be quiet. Yet this doesn't teach the toddler to behave on his or her own volition. It only teaches the opposite in fact. In other words, it teaches the child that if he or she misbehaves, the toddler will receive a gift or treat of some kind. Obviously, this is the wrong kind of attention for the little one. Rewarding bad behavior just reinforces it to happen again. This is not positive parenting but something else entirely.

In the same vein, rewarding misbehavior isn't good nor optimal for all parties involved because the toddler later in life as an adult will continue that misbehavior and still expect something from it like some kind of compensation for it. Yet if mom or dad stop rewarding their toddler's misbehavior, hopefully, the little one will change the misbehavior into something better due to the the extinction effect. In addition, rewarding a toddler's misbehavior doesn't teach much except that he or she will get a reward for being naughty. Makes no sense or logic, but there it is. It is almost like a form of operant conditioning, which is a learning process in which a behavior is changed through reinforcement and punishment. Yet conditioning a child to not act in his or her best interest is very destructive and unhealthy for both the child and the parent(s). In fact, rewarding misbehavior will likely hurt everyone involved, due to the negative outcomes resulting from it.

It is also common for parents and caretakers of children to criticize them personally when they misbehave and act out of turn. Yet if the criticism comes from the person closest to the child like mom or dad, the toddler can take this to heart. This has the effect of weakening the bond between parent and child, given the criticism in this form is a personal attack. Yet if the child's misbehavior, instead of the child, is constructively criticized gently and thoughtfully by his or her caretaker, perhaps the toddler will be more likely to take it into consideration. This is because he or she won't feel personally criticized or censured. Sometimes it can be very challenging to take constructive criticism even as an adult, which is why it is important to begin the process now when children are generally more open to everything including constructive criticism.

Clearly, the discipline mistakes typical of new parents are:

- Misunderstanding the purpose of discipline
- Overreacting to every little thing
- Lack of explanation
- Overusing punishment
- Empty threats
- Nagging
- Misusing time-outs
- Bribery
- Rewarding misbehavior
- Criticizing the child and not the behavior

It is okay to make discipline mistakes as long as parents and caretakers learn from them and then change their disciplining behavior into something more healthy for the child's sake and well-being; positive parenting and discipline with love no matter what. Healthy discipline is for the sake of the child's well-being and not the parent(s). In fact, positive parenting and discipline are to help the child have the best life possible now and in the future, because the lessons the child learns now will hopefully stay with him or her for a lifetime. The toddler as an adult, in turn, will then be able to positively parent and discipline his or her own children someday, too, and this will create healthy generations of family for years to come. This technique of parenting has a positive ripple effect on society as well, as family units are created in school, in the workplace, in church and even in bowling teams.

Chapter Seven:
Positive Parenting Tips For Toddlers

Positive parenting tips for toddlers need to be more dependent upon the toddler's development stage and not his or her age because although age is a static thing, development for toddlers is not; they are constantly evolving and changing right before our very eyes. A toddler's developmental growth accomplishments can occur many times during a given age resulting in him or her reaching development stage-appropriate milestones within a short amount of time. It is not fair to generalize a toddler and his or her age group because that just categorizes and stereotypes the toddler's behavior and abilities without really looking at what the toddler is capable of in his or her individual development stage. In short, parents need to familiarize themselves with this knowledge before thinking about how to positively parent his or her little one.

Parenting Tips and Reasons to Stay Positive

Once the parents or caretakers have this vital working knowledge of toddlers' abilities dependent on things like emotional, physical, and psychological development and growth, it is also important that the toddler's caretakers put this knowledge to good use to figure out what the toddler is capable of at this stage. This knowledge and parenting tip will dictate what is doable regarding what the parent can and cannot undertake with regard to a plan of action for parenting the toddler. For example, toddlers don't possess a whole lot of control over their own lives, given their lack of maturity at such a young age. This is why mom and dad need to take control for the toddler regarding things like teaching the toddler valuable lessons emanating from the guidance, structure, and discipline with unconditional love no matter what and even if.

Positive parenting tips and their reasons can be challenging to implement when our toddlers test and push our buttons. It can be hard to positively parent a child when he or she is throwing a tantrum for whatever reason, too. Yet it is important to remember as parents that it is our job to unconditionally love them no matter what and even if. This positive parenting tip is vital to remember because even if the child vocalizes his or her feelings about the parent for enforcing a discipline moment, the parent must still love him or her. Even if the child throws his or her toys at the parent(s), the parent must still love him or her. Even if the child hits the parent, the parent must still love him or her. It is important that the parent loves the child no matter what and even if because the toddler will benefit from that unconditional love more than any other aspect of parenting. For example, the child will benefit emotionally knowing mom or dad is there for him or her and the child will benefit physically because loving home environments help the child's brain to develop optimally. In short, unconditional love is a helpful positive parenting tip and the best medicine for the child.

Another aspect to consider via staying positive is that toddlers don't quite yet use or employ their minds the same way adults do because they lack the ability to engage in sophisticated thinking with things like logic and complex reasoning. A toddler's thinking ability is very simple and corporeal as a result, focusing on things they can touch, see, hear, taste, etc. Similarly, it is important to use simple but direct language with the toddler as his or her language capabilities are still developing. For example, try not to use compound sentences or complex directives because the toddler can't process sequences like this yet. What the toddler can do is string together simple phrases like "my toy". In order for the toddler to understand a directive from his or her caretaker, the adult should also use similar language, especially when implementing a limit or consequence by the means of discipline.

> **Quick Tip:** Label simple and safe objects in the house that the toddler can identify to enrich his or her language capabilities and skills.

It can be challenging to stay positive when disciplining but toddlers need to be disciplined in a healthy, balanced manner; otherwise, the toddler could end up in a worse life situation later down the road as an adult. For example, a toddler not being disciplined when the opportunity presents itself could result in an adult who doesn't listen to other authority figures like the police. On the other hand, too much discipline could land the toddler in a military training school like West Point. There needs to be a balance when disciplining the child because this will ultimately teach, guide and structure the child's life into the best life possible for him or her. In addition, healthy discipline as a positive parenting tip will create toddlers that can someday govern themselves appropriately. In fact, psychology research shows time and again that children need love and healthy discipline to become stable adults.

A good pointer for parenting positively is ensuring limits and consequences are easier to follow and understand when the toddler is given choices from mom or dad regarding them. Therefore, it is crucial to propose to the toddler the idea of choices, options or alternatives. This is partially because toddlers will feel they have more control over their own lives when given a choice as opposed to an ultimatum from his or her caretaker. Choices also help the toddler to feel more independent and confident. This is helpful when disciplining the toddler, too, because the toddler might be more likely to comply with mom's or dad's request as a result of being given two choices the caretakers are okay with. In addition, the toddler will learn through mom's or dad's carefully chosen options that he or she will have to deal with a consequence regarding that chosen option or choice. This teaches the toddler things like cause and effect and accountability for his or her actions. In short, choices help the toddler learn, through a process of operant conditioning, the better option regarding consequences.

A reason to look on the bright side of parenting

is that learning is taking place all the time when a child is a toddler. A toddler observes everything in his or her environment, especially the behaviors of his or her caretakers. In addition, whatever the caretakers do on a day-to-day basis, the toddler will eventually mirror them. As a result, it is important to model a positive demeanor and tone of voice when around the little one. This is especially true when disciplining the toddler because he or she will be less likely to react, think or feel negatively about it. In fact, it arguably takes more energy to be negative, especially when disciplining the toddler. On the other hand, when mom, dad or the caretaker is positive, he or she still has energy left after the teachable moment to give to the toddler emotionally. In short, save the emotion for the relationship with the toddler and not the discipline.

Yet discipline is only part of positive parenting,

because it is also vital for the toddler's caretaker(s) to model positivity in other areas of the toddler's life as well. This tip is important because then the little one might think and feel more positively about the world and his or her little corner of it in general. This positivity will benefit the toddler in many ways, too; including psychological, physical and emotional gains because the mind, body and emotions are all interconnected thus beneficially affecting the toddler. In short, if the toddler is usually a positive child, then he or she is probably a healthy child.

A healthy child requires mom or dad being willing to learn how to be a better parent to him or her by learning some of the basic principles of positive parenting and then applying them to particular stages of development. For example, since toddlers are at a development stage that is basically ground-level given they have just begun to grow and develop, two to three-year-old children don't possess much of an attention span quite yet. In fact, it is best to remember that the span of attention a toddler possess equates to about his or her physical age, so for a two-year-old, this is about two minutes. This is important for parents to remember when disciplining the toddler because if you spend ten minutes chastising him or her for breaking a limit or rule, the toddler will only remember the first few moments of your attempts at healthy discipline anyway. Yet if you can keep the momentum going when trying to teach and discipline the toddler, there is a higher chance that the toddler will remember more than if you just yelled at him or her because the toddler will be more engaged in the act of learning something from the discipline. In short, it is important to keep the child engaged in order for him or her to learn something new.

> **Quick Tip:** Make the first few minutes of a discipline opportunity count by emphasizing with your voice what it is you want the toddler to understand.

Clearly, learning something new on the toddler's part requires the caretaker to switch it up every few minutes to keep the child engaged in the activity. For example, if you and the child together are drawing shapes with crayons on a piece of paper, perhaps color the shapes in after a few minutes. Another example is if you and the child are sponge painting on big pieces of paper, perhaps switch up the shapes of the sponges every few minutes to keep it interesting to the toddler. The point is that the toddler will enjoy the activity even more than just doing one mundane activity at a time. Keep it fresh and exciting!

In addition, another tip for parenting with a positive attitude is that engaging with the toddler has the effect of mom or dad eventually thinking like their toddler the more they play with him or her. Next thing you know, the parent will also be amazed by things such as the color of that flower or feel of sand in his or her fingertips. This is advantageous to both the toddler and the parent because then the caretaker can better comprehend the inner workings of his or her toddler's mind, and thus be a better parent to him or her as a result. This is because the parent's approach of thinking like his or her toddler has the effect of the parent getting down to the child's level or developmental phase resulting in the little one hopefully being more receptive to mom or dad when it counts regarding positive parenting and discipline.

Staying upbeat as a parent is easier when you take care of yourself first. Otherwise, the caretaker of the child will not be in a position to positively parent the toddler with unconditional love no matter what. If the caretaker of the toddler has issues with taking care of him or herself for whatever reason, then his or her toddler's well-being which is dependent on the caretaker will also fall by the wayside. Whatever the parent has to do to restore a sense of balance, inner peace or normalcy, do not hesitate to do it. For example, the parent taking care of him or herself could ask a close friend to babysit for a few hours to get a momentary break. This will aid the parent in feeling more restored to once again take on the awesome task of positive parenting.

Clearly there are many positive parenting tips to help mom or dad navigate parenting their toddler, and some of those tips are:

- Familiarize yourself with knowledge on toddlers
- Love them unconditionally
- Understand toddlers have simplistic thinking
- Remember discipline must be balanced
- Give toddler choices
- Save energy for relationship with toddler and not the discipline
- Model positivity yourself
- Learn basic principles of positive parenting
- Keep momentum going via discipline
- Think like a toddler
- Take care of yourself

Self-care Tips

Parents need self-care in order to parent their toddlers the best he or she can in any given moment or situation. Self-care is vital because when parents feel better as a result of engaging in activities like a hot bubble bath, they can be there for their toddlers even more than if parents downplayed the need to engage in self-care. Self-care can be challenging though because as parents, the natural inclination is to take care of the children first. This is when parents have to consciously plan self-care into their schedule to make it a reality. Even if self-care means taking a ten-minute break in the bathroom to center oneself, be intentional about it. Since opportunities for self-care may be minimal given the mammoth task of positive parenting, work it into the day by doing small things to boost your level of self-care while the toddler is engaged in something else like playing with his or her toys on the floor. In fact, it would seem self-care is even more challenging because parents need to monitor their toddler twenty-four seven.

It is understandable that constantly keeping an eye on the toddler makes it hard for the parent to have some alone time. This favorable positive parenting tip is necessary because being alone allows parents to recharge their batteries and put things into perspective. On the other hand, it is also important for the parent(s) to discover the means to connect with other adults. This is also important because doing so gives the parent what he or she needs as a person. It is vital for adults to have relationships with other adults, in addition to their children.

The parent may take care of him or herself even better by joining or even establishing a community of like-minded individuals that are similar to the parent in some shape or form. For example, mom or dad could join a community of parents who also have toddlers at the same development stage. This would allow the parents in the community to relate to one another through coffee, shared stories and even play dates. It helps mom or dad to socialize with other adults because then he or she will be better equipped to handle positive parenting given mom or dad gets what he or she needs through connection with other human beings. Communities are also important because they give people a sense of belonging to something bigger than him or herself.

Another advantageous parenting tip is that this sense of belonging is also helpful to toddlers because he or she will be able to socialize and play more with other children, resulting in increased development socially and cognitively to name a few.

Quick Tip: Join your toddler during playtime to help him or her develop the social skills necessary to play with other children through modeling behaviors such as sharing yourself.

It is also important to try to stay positive as a parent because all too often, it is easy for parents to get bogged down by the everyday responsibilities of raising a child given realities pertaining to food, rent and even finding a babysitter. Yet having fun is necessary for mental, emotional and physical health, in part because doing so uplifts your spirit and sense of wellness and joy. Otherwise, depression and similar feelings could possibly set in, resulting in the parent being less likely to guide and discipline the child in a positive and healthy way. This can easily be avoided by engaging in activities that make you smile and bring to you a sense of happiness. In addition, having more fun will also bring more joy into your child's world because the parent will be smiling and laughing more. Happiness is contagious, and one idea for having fun is to perhaps go out with the girls or the guys one night to let your hair down. It took me a very long time to do this when my son was born, in part because I was a new mother. Be that as it may, it is important for the parent(s) to have fun and laugh because he or she will be a better parent with his or her toddler as a result.

Additionally, it would be very wise to also take care of your team or community because they will hopefully take care of you in turn as one of their own. A family member, a friend or even a church pastor can be part of the team to look after the parent and his or her toddler. In addition, if your team or community includes your toddler's daycare teachers, extended family or your spouse, make sure to establish and work on improving the relationships with them because they can help the parent or the toddler in one form or another when and if needed. They could help with things like babysitting, or just sharing his or her parenting experiences and advice with the toddler's parent. This team in effect creates a bigger group of people that look after each other. This is beneficial and has the ripple effect of everybody within the team looking out for one another, almost like an extended familial unit of sorts. It would also seem that belonging in the team or community helps to positively parent the child because it does indeed take a community to raise a child after all.

An important self-care tip to promote positive parenting is to play some enjoyable music because it can enhance or improve one's mood and outlook through the melodious expression of musical instruments and song. Music has positive benefits for the parent(s) because it can actually change one's mood. Therefore it is a good idea to play music for the mood you desire, like upbeat music for the energy to clean the toddler's bedroom. The caretaker could also play music to relax him or herself if stressed. In addition, the toddler will also positively benefit from the music.

It would at first seem odd that positive parenting tips for toddlers include self-care for mom and dad, but it is a necessary ingredient to produce a happy, well-balanced child.

Self-care for mom or dad can also include finding a hobby that he or she enjoys. For example, I like to bead. Some people like to paint. Whatever it is that makes the parent(s) happy by the means of engaging in a creative outlet, go for it. It is almost therapeutic to engage in a hobby because it allows the person to express themselves in a fun, healthy way.

Journaling about one's day can be an empowering way to regain a sense of self through expression of one's feelings and experiences throughout the day. Journaling can be also helpful because it allows the parent to write about what is on his or her mind in the moment instead of ruminating about it for hours on end.

Furthermore, it is also fun to engage in exercise on a regular basis. If the parent can make time in his or her busy schedule for exercise, the benefits of engaging in a physical activity will become obvious. This is because the parent will feel fit and more confident as a person. This in turn will help the parent to manage positive parenting, as regular exercise can be an outlet for stress as well. Exercise is like a natural antidepressant. It is clearly worth the effort to be active on a daily basis.

An additional great tip for positively parenting toddlers by the means of the caretaker's self-care is to pay it forward. This means engaging in a random act of kindness regularly. For example, the parent could offer to babysit her friend's toddler to give the other parent a break. This kind act will increase gratitude and thankfulness, in addition to bolstering positive feelings as a result of doing something good for somebody else.

Self-care also involves allowing yourself to experience emotion and feelings in such a way that you do not downplay their existence by busying yourself as a parent. For example, it is natural to sometimes feel bummed over the less than fun aspects of parenting. Yet don't allow the emotion to take precedence so much that function declines. This is why we have to express emotion in a healthy way to maintain our ability to be the best parent possible for the little one. However, feeling bummed can be countered by doing the things that make you smile and enjoy life. Another self-care tip for the caretaker to be a more positive parent is to simply get outside and go for a walk. A walk outside can do wonders for the soul and for the body because of the fresh air, sunshine and exercise. Sometimes a change in scenery can uplift the parent's mood, too.

Clearly, there are many self-care tips for parents of toddlers, and some of the more pertinent ones are:

- Intentionally plan self-care
- Have alone time
- Connect with other adults
- Establish a community
- Try to stay positive
- Have fun
- Take care of community
- Play Music
- Get outside
- Find a hobby
- Journaling
- Exercise
- Pay it forward

Tips On Being Patient with Toddlers

Enjoying life also requires mom or dad to be more patient with the kids as a positive parenting tip. If the caretaker is patient with his or her toddler, this allows mom or dad to think more clearly and to make better decisions regarding the toddler and his or her well-being. In order for mom or dad to be more patient with the toddler, it is important that he or she learns something about child development first to understand what is the norm regarding behaviors for that specific age group or development stage. This will allow the caretaker to be more understanding and thus patient of the toddler.

Being patient with one's toddler as a positive parenting tip also requires the caretaker to picture his or her toddler in about twenty years as an adult making his or her own choices for themselves. To explain, we sometimes lose patience when our toddler doesn't make a choice we try to force on them in the moment. Yet if mom or dad can understand that a toddler's choices are indeed his or her choices that will someday determine where and how he or she ends up in twenty years, this will allow mom or dad to have more patience with the child in the long run as well.

Another positive but patient parenting tip for toddlers is for mom or dad to put people before problems. This means the toddler's caretaker values the child more than what the child can or can't do at any given moment depending on the task set out for him or her. After all, the child is priceless in comparison to a clean room. In short, don't focus on the to-do list for the child, but focus on the child him or herself.

Being patient with toddlers also requires mom or

dad to find the fun. For example, instead of getting stressed out over the toddler spilling toothpaste on his or her new outfit, maybe discover what is funny in that moment. This will help the caretaker to be more patient with the child as he or she learns to laugh with the child. Laughing with the child sometimes helps mom or dad be more childlike as well in his or her approach with the toddler. Being more childlike allows the caretaker to better understand the child, this increasing patience with a better understanding of toddlers.

Being patient with toddlers is a skill easily learned if mom or dad just follows these tips:

- Learn about child development
- Picture toddler in twenty years making his or her own choices
- Put people before problems

- Find the fun or funny in everyday moments

One of the most important qualities a parent of a toddler needs is patience. Remembering the need for patience and employing a strategy to help you keep it in more stressful situations with your toddler will allow you to positively parent and to increase the joy inherent in positive parenting with unconditional love no matter what and even if. It is a joy to watch kids grow and with enough positive parenting tips, guidance and structure, parents can also enjoy the process as well with a little practice and effort. After all, children don't stay children forever. Enjoy the moments and memories while you can because once they are older, the toddler's life will be affected by what you do now regarding positive parenting and discipline.

Final Words

A parent's tough love is necessary to produce a capable, self-governing adult through years of hard work and careful planning. Likewise, maybe human beings do come with a set of instructions after all, via the positive parenting and discipline guidelines in this book. However, what isn't planned for is the ever-evolving emotional connection between parent and child. This connection is what reminds us that it is also okay to sometimes just be in the moment to experience the joy all around us without checking it off on the to-do list like another errand. In fact it would seem this joy counterbalances the exhaustive effort of raising another human being day in and day out. It just seems that as much as we try to plan for everything like parenting, life has a way of reminding us that sometimes the best plan is actually no plan.

Life happens whether we make plans for it or not. In addition, we can't always predict how things are going to go as parents and caretakers because children are always changing and evolving from one minute to the next. This unpredictability regarding our offspring suggests children are uninhibited and freer in thought and expression, in part because they haven't been affected by the world quite yet. However, this carefree and natural state of a child's existence is the reason for the literature on the subject everywhere. Ironically, the reason for the literature is to also train the wild child into a responsible controlled adult. Yet if this is the case, then why is the obsession with the fountain of youth so prevalent? Perhaps it is because as adults, it is easy to forget what it was like to be a child full of energy and life.

Although the energy and life-force of a child cannot be controlled, it can be molded and shaped into something resembling self-control and self-discipline via years of training the child to behave in accordance to what the powers that be deem appropriate at the time. Yet much time is needed for this discipline training because as the child changes throughout the years, so does the approach because it has to match the child's stage of development. The approach is everything because it is what shapes the child's actions and thinking now and in the future. Psychologists know that the thought processes of a responsible adult can probably be traced back to his or her developmental years when he or she was still forming into a coherent and conscious human being with thoughts and feelings of his or her own.

These thoughts and feelings are taken into consideration in the child-centered approach to positive parenting and discipline. In fact, this style of parenting is done with unconditional love no matter what. This is advantageous to the child because it will improve his or her psychological, physical, and emotional health and well-being in many ways. This well-being clearly stems from the structure and guidance in a responsive and nurturing home environment. In other words, environment is everything when it comes to giving the child the love, freedom and boundaries he or she needs to thrive.

Yet freedom and boundaries are harder to obtain without positive communication by the means of a reciprocal expression of words and body language between parent and child to understand one another during a teachable discipline moment. This discipline moment usually results from the child wanting to curiously explore his or her home environment and the parent wanting to ensure the child's safety and well-being. In short, a compromise can be reached if the parent and the child have not only a loving relationship but also a working relationship that allows for room to individually grow and develop.

However, a compromise should never occur regarding one's self-care because without it, positive parenting can go downhill fast given mom's and dad's well-being is diminished resulting in the child also not receiving the best care. Be that as it may, the care of the child is paramount in order for him or her to have the best life possible via the structure, guidance and discipline inherent in positive parenting. Parenting and nurturing oneself via a personal respite speaks volumes as well.

Also speaking volumes is the parent's effortful attempts to positively parent the child because it takes a conscious, purposeful and intentional effort to learn new techniques of parenting while also not repeating history with our own parents' parenting styles. In fact, learning a new parenting style like positive parenting also requires a mindfulness of sorts given it takes repeated practice to master.

Mastering the many positive parenting tips and advice in this book is helpful to the parent(s) or caretakers because it takes a lot of energy to unconditionally love their child no matter what and even if. Tips such as getting down to the child's level to appear less imposing as an adult are helpful when trying to structure, guide and discipline the child with empathy and love. In addition, advice such as giving the child alternative choices or options to avoid discipline become useful when mom or dad is trying to balance parenting with other life responsibilities like work. Yet the biggest responsibility and privilege I can think of is loving and disciplining the child in order for him or her to have the best life possible.

The key to learning positive parenting is clear,

and that is to practice the tips and advice in this book regularly. In short, don't just read the book and then do nothing. Take action to improve your child's life and well-being one positive parenting tip at a time. Actually embody and practice the positive parenting mantra as well to love the child no matter what and even if. Just remember that the love you give your child is unconditional, selfless and altruistic, meaning it is for the benefit of the child and his or her well-being in order to have the best life possible now and in the future.